Pelican Book

Crime in a Changing Society

Howard Jones is now Professor of Social
Administration at the University College,
Cardiff. Before taking up a university
appointment, he worked for some years as a
social worker, mainly in residential institutions
for delinquent and problem children. The fruit of
that experience was a book, *Reluctant Rebels*,
published in 1961. Apart from his interest in
crime and other forms of deviance (he is the
author of the only British textbook of
criminology, and of a book on *Alcoholic
Addiction*), his present work has been concerned
with the theory of small groups and of social
organizations. He has initiated a series of
experiments in the training of social workers for
work with groups, and is currently engaged in
research on the application of this idea to the
understanding of correctional schools, hospitals,
prisons, etc.

Dr Jones has also lectured in the United
States, and in Canada at the University of
Toronto. He is married and has one small son.

Crime in a Changing Society

Howard Jones

Penguin Books

Penguin Books Ltd, Harmondsworth,
Middlesex, England
Penguin Books Inc., 7110 Ambassador Road,
Baltimore, Maryland 21207, U.S.A.
Penguin Books Australia Ltd, Ringwood,
Victoria, Australia

First published 1965
Reprinted with revisions 1967
Reprinted 1970, 1971
Copyright © Howard Jones, 1965, 1967

Made and printed in Great Britain by
Hazell Watson & Viney Ltd,
Aylesbury, Bucks

Set in Linotype Pilgrim

Contents

Introduction

At the present time there is more stealing than ever before, more destruction of both private and public property, and more important, perhaps, a large increase in crimes of violence against the person. Crimes of violence are still relatively few in total; it is the trend which is disturbing. We are unlikely, of course, to be unaware of these facts. The press gives plenty of space to crime, and very much more space to crimes of violence and sex than their importance in the total picture could justify. Many newspapers are less concerned with supplying news than with attracting readers; and as far as news of crime is concerned, this means appealing to the interest we have, for private reasons of our own, in violence and sex.

We are entitled to a more objective picture and it is part of the purpose of this book to try to provide it. In the science of criminology, crime and criminals are subjected to the sober and objective study that is necessary for this task. A disinterested attitude towards crime, however, is not easy to achieve. In the first place, our emotions and our own sense of inner security are implicated: and nothing makes more for biased judgements than emotional involvement. But this is only part of the story. Intricately interwoven with our emotional needs, but playing in their own right an essential role in our lives, are our personal moralities and our sense of justice. To study crime objectively seems to deny both of these, for it is to treat 'bad behaviour' as 'just behaviour'.

Criminologists come from many professional backgrounds. They may be psychologists, physiologists, lawyers, philosophers, sociologists, or historians. They tackle the problem with specialized skills but a common purpose: to understand the phenomena and the causes of criminal deviance.

This is also the way in which society, and the victims of the criminal, may best be defended. To cure a disease, we need first to know something about it. Just as a pain, though unpleasant, is no more than a symptom of an underlying process of disease, so crime may be the outward indication that something more fundamental is going wrong. These personal and social ills may be the things which really matter, rather than the more obtrusive fact of increasing criminal behaviour.

This book, then, sets out to introduce the reader to a scientific approach to the crime problem and also to suggest some new ways of combating it. The first chapter attempts an assessment of the size of the problem. This is less straightforward than it sounds; the figures published in Blue Books and quoted so freely by press and government are incomplete and probably distorted. Before one can even start to study crime, it is necessary to appreciate how imprecise is much of the data with which one has to work. Figures, in criminology as elsewhere, give an impression of certainty which is not justified by the nature of the information on which they are based. 'Understanding the figures' is therefore an essential first step.

Chapters 2 to 5 are concerned with the understanding of causes. In Chapter 2 some possible sociological causes will be examined; and Chapter 3 will ask, and try to answer, a question which has often been asked, and answered (in various ways), before: are criminals born criminal, or made so by their experience? This is a vital question, for if criminality is inborn, the implications, for treatment and prevention, are fatalistic and very grim.

Chapters 4 and 5 deal with the moulding of the criminal personality by the environment of family and community within which it matures. If causes have to be seen as residing in personal abnormality, as something more than the response of the normal person to his surroundings, an approach like this provides the only alternative to the fatalism of hereditarian theories. Then in Chapter 6, an attempt is made to bring together the various kinds of causal factor (personal and social) discussed in earlier pages, in order to try to discover how they combine to produce criminal behaviour. In the same chapter the ways in which society may deal with the criminal when he has been caught are briefly described as a preliminary to a more detailed examination of the penal system.

First to be dissected under this heading, in Chapter 7, must be our ideas about punishment for crime, together with the psychological sources from which these seem to spring. What is justice? How just can it be? Is real justice achievable, or ought it to be replaced by some other aim – like trying to cure? The courts, as the means through which we administer justice, must be affected by the answers given to questions like these, and the investigation undertaken in Chapter 8 may throw some doubt upon our traditional confidence in them.

But the courts are the gateway to the penal system. Since the war with Hitler, many new ways of dealing with criminals have been developed. Nevertheless they fall still into two broad groups: those which involve sending the offender away from home to a residential institution, like prison, borstal, or the approved school, and those which, like probation, try to deal with him while he is living with his family, and in his normal environment. Chapter 9, in dealing with penal institutions, breaks with the old convention of assuming that the influence of the staff of an institution upon the inmates is almost all that matters. Our penal institutions are not very successful, and their success rates are declining, so that at present, out of every three boys committed to borstal, almost two are convicted of further offences after discharge. One of the reasons for the poor record of residential penal methods (as forms of correctional treatment, at any rate) may be the gross oversimplification involved in the view already mentioned that they are merely places in which staff do things to and for inmates. They are communities, like other communities, in which the relationships of inmates between themselves, and of staff between themselves, cannot be left out of account.

The discussion in Chapter 10 must also cover a wide field. Although probation is by far the most important element in our present programme of correction outside institutions, and although it is, as far as it goes, a progressive and valuable tool, it does not go far enough. It tends to overlook the wider social context within which people live. Chapter 10 sees an important future for probation, but as one part of a many-pronged attack on the roots of the crime problem in the community and the group, as well as in the individual.

The last two chapters of the book meditate further upon this social theme. They ask, to begin with, what recent trends in crime imply for our society. What does the post-war wave of teenage crime and teenage violence really amount to, has it no further meaning, or could it be a pointer to the way in which our society itself is drifting? The quest for causes is probably an ultimate one, and like most ultimate tasks, it may be unachievable. Far short of that, we may be able to take some action to improve our social condition, drawing from research into the causes of crime but seeking to do very much less than attempt to remove them all. Activity of this kind may seem limited, but it is at least practical.

Chapter 1

Understanding the Figures

Crime is on the increase throughout the Western world. In particular juvenile delinquency of a disturbingly violent and senseless kind is flaring up throughout Europe and North America. In the United States, over two million serious crimes were reported in 1962 – a six per cent rise (twice the percentage increase during the previous year) over the all-time high of 1961. The F.B.I. report from which these figures were taken continues: 'Crime in the last five years increased four times faster than population. Four serious crimes per minute recorded on the crime clock.' The Americans, it seems, have reason to feel worried about their crime problem. The increase may be a little lower in this country, but with a rate of serious convictions in 1965 higher than ever before, implicating more than double the proportion of the population involved in crime before the war, we have no cause for complacency.

But perhaps the greater danger is that we may be panicked into measures of repression which will do more damage to our system of social values than the crime itself. How a society treats its offenders is an index of its basic attitude towards human personality; if, for instance, we ill-treat our thieves, we show only too clearly what we put first, property or people.

It is also only too easy for us to be misled about how much crime really occurs; and our usual tendency is to overestimate rather than to minimize the problem. A string of sadistic murders occur, and all at once the streets are hardly safe to walk in any more. A couple of people we know have their houses broken into, and all at once burglars are everywhere, creeping around darkened gardens, or 'casing the joint' in broad daylight. Perhaps the best illustration of our tendency to exaggerate our crime problem is to be found in recent public attitudes towards murder. Not long ago there was a quick succession of brutal sex murders. Little girls and one or two women were raped and then killed. Public anxiety and indignation about this reached a climax, and there were many demands, both in the press and elsewhere, for the restoration of the death penalty, abolished for certain kinds of murder in 1957. Popular clamour led to research by the Home Office into the number of murders committed over recent years, with results which hardly justified some of the extreme statements being made. The proportion of homicides, in relation to population, committed in 1960 was actually less than in 1957, and only fractionally more than before the war.

The amount of anxiety evoked by crime, and especially violent crime, is such that one is tempted to feel that its roots lie deep. We are, of course, bound to be impressed by striking examples of criminal behaviour in our society, but why are such very strong feelings aroused in us? Why, for example, in the face of criminal violence, do we ourselves become so violent in return? When a particularly brutal act is committed, people say 'I wish I could get my hands on him', with a vehemence that, in cooler moments, makes us realize just how precarious is our control over our own more violent emotions. It may be, in other words, because a shadowy unacknowledged side of ourselves finds criminal behaviour not uncongenial, that we are so upset when it breaks through in other people.

The more serious our crime problem is, the more important it is that we should look at it coolly and rationally. If crime is becoming a real threat, we cannot afford the luxury of indulging our feelings. The first step is obviously to determine how serious the problem really is. Published statistics are available, and they are our only really firm source of information on this subject, but they must not be taken at their face value, for they depend to a considerable extent upon the activities of the police. The police are not unresponsive to public pressure, and at times of rising criminality there is a tendency for them to become more severe. As a study in Liverpool by Bagot has shown, fewer offenders receive cautions at such a time; and where there is a choice, the police tend also to bring prosecutions under the more serious rather than the less serious headings. Behaviour of this kind, while perfectly understandable, is bound to exaggerate any increase which is actually taking place. An epidemic of offences of a rather disturbing kind is also, as we have seen, likely to lead to a public outcry, and to increased police activity. The rash of prosecutions for homosexual behaviour in this country a few years ago was almost certainly partly attributable to this cause; a few well-publicized cases of homosexuality among prominent people led to much more vigilance on the part of the police, leading to still more arrests, and all at once standards of public decency seemed to be desperately threatened.

Changes in the law have much the same effect. The Street Offences Act 1959 has almost certainly caused an increase in the number of prosecutions for offences connected with prostitution, but it is an artificial increase, which gives no real indication of whether the number of prostitutes is larger or smaller than it was before the Act was passed. When it became clear that the police were determined to enforce the Act, prostitutes, not surprisingly, went to ground. It would therefore be mere guesswork for the visitor to London, who finds himself no longer accosted on Charing Cross Road, to assume that there has been any real diminution in this problem because of the prosecutions. The more recent Betting and Gaming Act, 1960, has reduced the number of prosecutions for street bookmaking to vanishing point, without involving any change in social behaviour at all. The decline in criminal statistics on this count is due simply to the fact that behaviour which was previously illegal is now permitted.

All this demonstrates how imperfect criminal statistics are, in spite of their apparent objectivity, as a reflection of the actual picture. In evaluating them one must in the first place distinguish very clearly between the number of 'findings of guilt' (or, slightly differently, the number of 'persons found guilty') and the number of crimes known to the police. The former include only those crimes that the police have been able to solve, and to prove in a court of law. They represent the very smallest available measure of our crime problem. The figure of crimes known to the police is always very much larger : in the year 1965 it was nearly four times as large as the total number of offences for which individuals were actually convicted in the same year. This is partly because the police, in certain circumstances, issue a formal caution to an offender instead of prosecuting him. In recent years, about one in eight or one in nine of our more serious offenders have been dealt with in this way, nearly a third of the boys under fourteen, and nearly a half of the girls. That the police take into their own hands the duties of the judge as well as of the prosecutor, in this way, may give rise to misgivings in the minds of some but its importance for the purposes of the present chapter is that it makes our court figures very unrepresentative of the crime situation as a whole.

The other and more important cause of this discrepancy is the substantial proportion of offences which have been brought to the notice of the police in one way or another, but which they have been unable to clear up. The efficiency of our police forces is continually increasing, and they now have at their disposal many modern aids, such as forensic laboratories, wireless, and fast patrol cars; but modern offenders also keep up to date, and the complexity of life in modern urban centres as well as the sheer increase in the amount of crime being committed makes it easier for them to avoid detection. So the proportion of the offences known to the police which they have been able to clear up is declining; only one half of them were solved before the war, and the proportion has now fallen to less than forty per cent. It is somewhat startling to realize that such an offender has more than a fifty-fifty chance of getting off scot-free, but the police are in no way to be blamed for this state of affairs. The price of a high detection rate would be dear, if in its place we had to endure an arbitrary police force, with unrestricted rights of interrogation and arrest. It may be that a fairly large number of unsolved crimes is to be expected if we are to preserve our freedom in these respects.

But all this has to do only with those offences which are formally recorded, either in the records of our criminal courts or at the police station. What of the many informal cautions which must be issued : a blind eye which even an uncorrupt police service like ours must occasionally turn upon certain kinds of offence? And even more difficult to estimate : what of the many offences which never come to the notice of the police at all? This is the so-called 'Dark Number' of crime. One can only guess at its size. That it is a substantial number is certain.

Unrecorded crimes are likely to range all the way from the most trivial to the most serious. At the one extreme are the wordy conflicts often fought over back-garden fences, culminating sometimes even in blows. They rarely end in summonses for defamation or assault, and indeed a few days later the antagonists may be the best of friends, possibly even allies now against a common adversary. The courts never hear of these rifts; instead the husbands of the ladies concerned adjudicate upon the problem over a quiet pint in the public bar, coming to the invariable conclusion that, 'It's just these women. . . .' One might be inclined to feel that offences of this kind, if they can be called crimes at all, hardly matter, but comparable actions are recorded and presented as part of our crime picture. We have to remember how partial a picture it is.

We may jib at including back-yard squabbles, but (with the veneration we have for private property) would have no doubt that stealing is a crime. Many offenders against property are almost certainly never reported to the authorities. They may include, for instance, the chief clerk of a highly respected firm of family solicitors, who is tempted to defraud his employers after many years of blameless service. He may be a very efficient managing clerk, but as a criminal he is a mere novice, and the deficiencies in his accounts soon come to light. His employers have little to gain by prosecuting him; it could only bring them unwelcome publicity, and make their clients wonder if, having such a staff, they were quite as trustworthy as had been thought. Better by far not to prosecute : to dismiss the culprit and leave it at that. Regularly, older school children employed on Saturday mornings in a large department store in one of our great cities steal some of the goods temptingly placed at their disposal; they are admonished and threatened, and then sent home, for from the firm's point of view, it would be hardly worth preferring charges against them.

A recent study of employment prospects for ex-offenders, carried out by Dr J. P. Martin of the Cambridge Institute of Criminology, shows that this kind of unwillingness to prosecute is widespread in industry. Executives of forty-nine larger and forty-eight smaller firms, when interviewed in the course of the research, reported a total of ninety offences by their employees which involved the firm in some direct sense (stealing from the firm itself or its customers or from employees, assault at work, etc.), and of these only thirty-two or under thirty-six per cent were actually prosecuted. Even some of these prosecutions occurred apparently against the wishes of the firms, for the proportion in which they called in the police themselves was only twenty-eight per cent. The disappearance from sight of nearly two thirds of the crimes committed in these concerns is serious, but this is by no means all. For the number of offences occurring seems to be a good deal larger than the number which the firms actually recognize as offences.

There are two reasons for this. Many of the firms studied distinguished between 'pilfering' and stealing; the former, including the taking of items of small value – nails, screws, firewood, or a little paint in the building industry for instance – was ignored, and even expected. The extent to which this may happen is shown by a comment by one firm: 'What can you do when every department puts in a big order for brown paper at Christmas? It would cost more to stop than to condone.' This remark brings out the further point, that often, to avoid trouble and expense, firms covered by the study often did not maintain very efficient safeguards against stealing; of the total of eighty-seven firms, seventy-five felt that thieving from the firm would be easy.

In other words the total of ninety offences mentioned above is bound to be an underestimate, and thirty-two prosecutions to represent a much smaller proportion of this larger total than even thirty-six per cent. To fail to report crimes in this way is itself a crime. But there are more important considerations than this. For private industry to usurp the function of the courts in this arbitrary fashion is bad, whether one is mainly interested in the equitable administration of justice or in seeing that offenders receive the kind of treatment which will help them to keep out of trouble in the future.

Even murder may have a modest place in the Dark Number. In the light of recent researches on the possibilities of secret homicide (through the use of poisons for example) it is clear that murder can be committed and be passed off as natural death.

We have so many inhibitions about sex, and try to keep so much of the sexual side of human nature out of sight, that sexual offences of one kind and another are bound to find a fairly prominent place among those crimes that remain unrecorded and unacknowledged. The Street Offences Act 1959, for instance, as a fairly deliberate attempt to drive prostitutes off the streets, is certain in the long run to make offences of this kind very difficult to detect, and increase their share in the Dark Number. This is a case, moreover, in which the number of unacknowledged offences must already have been very large in relation to the number actually recorded. The earlier policy adopted by the police of charging prostitutes more or less in turn, meant that a woman could continue to practise her trade regularly, subject to an occasional informal tax, in the form of a fine. Every conviction thus stood as representative for a large mass of similar offences actually committed. The number of convictions for indecent behaviour between men has also greatly increased since the war but there are many clandestine liaisons of a homosexual kind, and even many stable 'marriages' between men, about which the law knows nothing. Even incest, hidden as it is within the family circle, is probably much commoner than the rather rare prosecutions for it would suggest.

In spite of the progress which has been made towards sexual freedom, we are, it seems, still too prudish to face up to much of the sexual behaviour that goes on around us. From the point of view of social hygiene, it is probably a very bad thing that we should drive our prostitutes off the street and our homosexuals into hiding, so that we can no longer make contact with them and either (according to one's social philosophy) try to cure them or to learn to live amicably beside them. But by such policies we certainly prevent ourselves from getting any real idea as to how prevalent sexual offences are.

Although, from the very nature of the Dark Number, it is impossible to attempt any real estimate of its size, one might guess that it is as much as four times that of crimes known to the police. As the number of crimes successfully prosecuted constitutes roughly one third of the latter figure, it is possible that only one crime in twelve ultimately ends in a sentence by the courts.

We cannot, of course, really know what this proportion is, but it is sufficiently large to render the court figure a rather small fraction of our total crime problem. And it is bound to be an unrepresentative fraction, since one kind of offence is much more likely to come to light, or to be detected, than another. A discreet homosexual relationship may never be discovered; a murder must be very well-planned indeed to escape notice. In these circumstances we are bound to be misled, if we rely upon official crime statistics, about the relative importance of different types of crime. As a further example, consider abortion. This is legal in Britain only if carried out under medical supervision, to protect the health (including the mental health) of the mother. Yet many unmarried girls, and many poor or hard-driven mothers of large families, succeed in terminating unwanted pregnancies every year. Occasionally, usually because something has gone wrong and the mother has to be treated in hospital, illegal operations of this kind are discovered, and the backstreet practitioner who carried it out (if found) is prosecuted. One hundred and forty of them were prosecuted in 1965, but no one would suggest that only 140 illegal abortions took place in that year. The police reports mention 184, and even this must be a tiny fraction of the whole.

Police forces also differ a good deal in their attitude to particular kinds of offences; this affects not only the kinds of things to which individual officers, and even the force as a whole, turn a blind eye, but also the kind of things for which a particular force is prepared to issue a formal caution rather than to prosecute. Any comparison of the prevalence of particular offences in different areas is likely to be affected by this. Uniformity in recording and cautioning policy has greatly improved since the war, but the local autonomy in our police service (which many see as a real safeguard for our liberties) is bound to lead to some degree of local variation.

Subject to these limitations it seems that convictions for crime (in proportion to population), both among juveniles and adults, is running at a level two and a half times as high as that immediately before the war. The greatest increase in numbers took place, as one might have expected, during the war years, but except for a downward trend during the first half of the fifties, the figures have risen steadily ever since. Both among juveniles and adults more offenders are now being convicted annually than at any other time in our history.

The figure for offences known to the police includes, as we have seen, a larger proportion of the total number of offences committed than does the figure of convictions; if this more complex index is used, the rate of increase has been even more rapid, the figure for 1965 being nearly four times as great as the figure over the period 1935–39. The important question, however, is what proportion this figure bears to the Dark Number. If the proportion of crimes known to the police has tended to increase, then this increase would exaggerate the increase that has actually occurred in crimes committed. Because the Dark Number consists of offences which are not reported, there can be no firm estimate of the proportion remaining undisclosed. We do know, however, that the proportion of those offences known to the police which they have been able to clear up has fallen, as compared with the pre-war proportion. This has no direct bearing upon the proportion to be found in the Dark Number, but shows that the police are having increasing difficulty in detecting offences, a difficulty which we might expect to see reflected in their ability to discover what crimes have occurred. In other words, although the number of crimes known to the police has increased so dramatically, the number of crimes actually occurring has probably increased to an even greater extent as compared with

1938, for 'crimes known' seems likely to form a diminishing proportion of the total committed.

Almost 1,133,882 serious offences were brought to the attention of the police in the year 1962. To look at the figures in another way, of every ninety people (men, women, and children, ten or over) in a dance-hall, a cinema or on the street, one will have been convicted of a serious offence during the previous twelve months. The number who have actually committed such an offence, irrespective of whether they have been prosecuted for it or not, would of course be much larger. And the number who have committed such an offence at some time during their lives (and not merely during the previous year) would be larger still.

All age groups have shared in this increase, but it has been most marked among teenagers. We have all been aware of disturbed behaviour among adolescents during the years since the end of the war, and it appears that this has been paralleled by a marked upward trend in delinquency among these age-groups.

It is only too easy to exaggerate this tendency; youth has always been going to the dogs, if older people are to be believed. (In fact the early teens *have* always been a period of high delinquency, but whereas the peak age used to be about thirteen for boys it is now about fifteen.) A further corrective against undue pessimism about youth is that only a small proportion of our adolescent offenders go on to become adult criminals. They sow their wild oats, but then apparently marry and settle down. This is not to underrate the nuisance value, or the criminal character of this large number of adolescent offences; they represent a serious problem in their own right, and some young offenders undoubtedly are confirmed in a life of crime by their experience at this age.

There has also been a shift in the kind of offences committed. Personal violence forms more than twice as large a proportion of the total number of offences known to the police as it did during the period 1935–39. Malicious injury to property increased even more strikingly to more than three times its pre-war proportion. Robbery is also over three times as important, in our total crime picture, as it was. Burglary and sex offences show a proportionately small increase, while offences against property without violence (various forms of stealing) have actually decreased in importance. In many ways this is striking confirmation of what most of us felt must have been happening. There has been an increase in personal violence and the destruction of property; yet this too must be seen in its proper perspective. The number of crimes of personal violence known to the police is still less than one fortieth of the serious offences reported to them, and the proportion of cases of malicious injury to property is even smaller, amounting to less than one in every hundred and fifty cases reported. Nearly three quarters of our serious offences are still simple stealing. It is very unlikely that these proportions would be altered very much by taking into account the offences hidden away in the Dark Number, for the vast majority of these must also be crimes of dishonesty.

One of the unsolved mysteries of criminology is the much lower rate of criminality among girls and women as compared with men. Although the extent of male superiority in this respect varies a little from country to country or from time to time, it has fluctuated at a figure of about eight to one in this country over recent years. As nothing is known about the personal characteristics (i.e. sex, age, etc.) of an offender until he has been detected and convicted, the figure of crimes known is useless for this purpose. We have to rely instead upon the court figures and these show that, for every female dealt with for a serious offence in this country, there are about eight males convicted. Why is this? The first attempt at an explanation of differences in the behaviour of men and women is usually of a biological kind. Alas for so simple an explanation! Social anthropologists, studying societies as far removed from ours in customs as they are in geography, have shown that many of the features of behaviour which distinguish the sexes in our culture are not essential differences of a biological kind at all, but derive from the needs and beliefs of the social group in question.

Men in our society seem to get into trouble more often because they are more exposed to the stresses and temptations of social life outside the home. Men go out more, and, being the breadwinners, are also subject to more powerful economic pressures than women. The more secluded women are by the customs of their country, the smaller their share of the country's crime. Women commit very few crimes in the Moslem countries of the Middle East, where they are often kept in purdah. Nor does this only apply where there are such extreme differences in the social position of men and women. In many rural areas in this country women are still more restricted in their social relationships than women living in the city. They are not only more protected than city women, but are also probably more subordinated. This has the result which might have been anticipated: a lower ratio of male to female crime in the city as compared with the country.

In order to explain striking features of our crime problem, like the sex-ratio, we often obtain most illumination from such an examination of the pattern of social life: the personal relationships we establish with one another, and the ideals and customs which our society upholds. Another example of this is the connexion between the seasons of the year and particular kinds of crime. It does seem to be established that (with certain exceptions) more crimes against property, such as stealing, burglary, etc., occur in the winter, while crimes of violence against the person tend to be crowded into the summer months. Quetelet, who first saw the value of applying statistical methods to the study of social questions like crime, argued over a hundred years ago that similar climatic factors accounted for the distribution of criminal behaviour between different parts of the world: property crimes predominated in the colder areas, and crimes against the person in the warmer. So confident was he about the universality of this connexion, that he described it as the 'Thermic Law of Crime'. Earlier, and even more sweepingly, Montesquieu put forward the proposition that criminal behaviour tended to predominate nearer the equator, and drunkenness nearer the polar regions. Needless to say, the reputation of his great book *L'Esprit des Lois* derives more from its contribution to political thought than to criminal climatology. A great Italian criminologist, Enrico Ferri, developed a more sophisticated theory: because less energy is used in the warmer weather, there is a surplus which is diverted into acts of violence. But such views as these are highly speculative, and based upon assumptions about human physiology for which there is no evidence. Simpler and more common-sense explanations are available, accounting for the seasonal distribution, at least, in social terms. After all, stealing is likely to be easier, in the northern hemisphere, during the long dark nights of winter; and people are out and about, mixing more during the summer, and are therefore more likely to quarrel and to fight.

All in all, we have to face up to the fact that crime is on the increase, and that it has increased on a very considerable scale as compared with pre-war times. People often talk about 'crime waves', and some may feel that what we are witnessing here is a crime wave. However, waves go down as well as up, whereas the general trend in our crime figures at the moment seems to be steadily upwards. One possibility is that what we are experiencing is not a passing phenomenon, but a continuing process of change in our way of life, in the course of which our customary ways of behaving and our traditional values are going to be radically modified.

Karl Mannheim argued that youth, entering adult life full of new ideas and rebellious impulses, was a major agency of social change. Certainly, the present increase in criminality is greatest among young people, whose share of the total seems to increase almost year by year. And ominously enough for the direction which social change (if such it is) seems to be taking, it is towards the more aggressive kind of offence that the increase seems to be slanted. Clear thinking about the causes of our current crime problem is going to be required if any progress is to be made in halting it. In the next chapter, possible causes arising out of the social life of neighbourhood communities will be explored. This will be followed by an examination of theories of inborn and inherited criminality, and an examination of innate factors (such as temperament or intelligence) which may contribute, if less directly, towards producing anti-social behaviour. Finally psychiatric causes, upon which so much stress is often laid nowadays, will receive attention.

Chapter 2

The Delinquent Subculture

Most great cities have their 'tough' neighbourhoods, in which women are warned not to walk alone after dark, and gossip has it that even policemen patrol in pairs, for fear of attack. Much of this is, of course, sheer mythology: the wild speculations of one section of society about another whose way of life is unknown, but obviously so different from its own as to seem vaguely threatening. If we have no factual information about other people, we are apt to endow them with whatever traits we are most anxious to deny in ourselves. This is a point which must be taken up later in the discussion of our attitude towards criminals, but it might be put, if rather dogmatically, in these words: the unknown (i.e. unconscious) in ourselves is undesirable and dangerous, and therefore the unknown elsewhere is also undesirable and dangerous. It is a small step from this position to one in which specific undesirable and dangerous things which are in us are seen as being in the unknown elsewhere, rather than in ourselves – a step which is easily taken because it relieves us of so much of the burden of our own worse side.

The popular belief about these neighbourhoods appears to receive striking confirmation from what is known about the proportion of their residents who are brought before the courts for criminal offences of one kind or another. They are the so-called delinquency areas, which have a much higher rate of criminality than more conventionally respectable localities.

In the past they have usually been deteriorated slum areas, and this has led to the belief that it is from their lack of amenities, and the poverty of their inhabitants, that their bad behaviour arises. Indeed, in the years between the wars, many people believed that all kinds of social problems – ill health, drunkenness, unemployability, etc. – arose from such causes, and that when people were rehoused and provided with a satisfactory livelihood, most of these problems would disappear. In its application to crime and delinquency, there has in the past been some evidence to support this view. It has been shown that in Britain, at any rate, adult crimes against property (though not against the person) tend to rise and fall in sympathy with the rate of unemployment – the more unemployment the more crime against property, and vice versa. According to studies carried out during the same period, there is also reason to believe that, among offenders in penal institutions, the rate of unemployment at the time they committed the offences for which they were sentenced was higher than that in the community at large. As the total work-history of these offenders was nevertheless average, some connexion between their unemployment and their offences would seem to be indicated.

But all this was during the inter-war years. Since the war we have had (relatively) full employment, and although real poverty is still commoner among certain under-privileged groups, like old-age pensioners, than some would have us believe, it is on the retreat. The slum clearance and rehousing programme, well under way before the war, also gained momentum, and in some towns the slum problem is virtually solved. Many former slum dwellers are now rehoused in pleasant municipal estates. But in spite of all these improvements, crime in this country is running at a higher level than ever before. And if further evidence is required, the United Nations, in a recent report, has pointed out that juvenile delinquency has tended to increase most in those countries of Europe in which the standard of life is highest – in the poorer countries of southern Europe it has increased hardly at all.

If there is a lesson which can be drawn from the apparent contradiction between our inter-war and post-war crime experience, it is that a factor, such as poverty, which may be of the greatest importance at one time, may at another time and under other social conditions be of no importance at all. Many factors seem to affect our crime position; if one wanes another may wax; Indeed, the very fact of change may be the important thing sometimes. The changes brought about by our increasing affluence present us with new problems, and these, in their turn, have their effect upon our crime figures.

Thus as populations have been transferred to new housing estates, the decaying slum areas, with their high crime rates, have been torn down; but in their places the new housing estates have become a problem for the police. Sometimes this lasts only for a few years, the delinquency rate on a new estate falling then to a more normal level, but this does not always happen, and some housing estates go from strength to strength, as it were, until they seem likely to challenge the shady record of the old slum area itself.

Even before the war, tendencies of this kind had been apparent, though not so obviously as to challenge the widespread belief in social amelioration as a cure-all. But not all respectable citizens were in agreement with this view; others, as they watched the rough and feckless residents of the slums being transferred to the new estates, realized at once that no good could come of it. The mythology of the no-good slum dweller was adapted to fit the no-good estate dweller, who kept his coals in the bath and his hens in the kitchen.

Now, it seems, we have almost reached full circle. Our slums are almost gone, our new housing estates are many and attractive. But we still have our delinquency areas, now located in the new estates, and so are not robbed of our scapegoats. The proof of their fecklessness is nowadays to be found in behaviour more in conformity with the living standards of the affluent society. They live in subsidized council houses, which they are said to neglect, while spending most of their money in deposits on such symbols of loose-living as cars, television sets, washing machines, and refrigerators.

But when all is said and done, there does seem to be a delinquency-areas problem. If, on a map of any of our cities, a spot is placed at the address of each offender brought before the court for a serious offence, the spots cluster in certain localities. This is not conclusive, for allowances have to be made for differences in population. To take an example obvious enough to make the point clear, it would hardly be sensible to compare the number of convicted offenders in the Metropolitan Police Area with the number in Redhill, Surrey; the number at risk of becoming delinquent is so much greater in the former case. Nevertheless a study by Morris of the distribution of criminality in Croydon in 1953 showed that convictions for serious offences varied in different parts of the borough from 0·09 per cent of the population to 0·75 per cent. In other words, one's chances of being convicted were eight and a half times as great if one lived in one area of the town rather than another.

A study of juvenile offences only, carried out in Leicester in the same year, showed that only 0·24 per cent of the juvenile population in one area had been found guilty of a serious offence, while in another area the proportion was 2·02 per cent. The risk of delinquency is therefore again between eight and nine times as great in the latter area as in the former. Delinquency areas clearly exist, and they tend to be either slums, or new housing estates.

One attempt by criminologists to explain this state of affairs assumes that the fault lies in some flaw in the community life of the delinquency area. The delinquency area, it is argued, is one in which community life is disintegrating. The old slum area is decaying, and people try to escape from it if they can. Slum clearance accelerates this process. Meanwhile it offers a refuge for new immigrants, who cannot afford high rents, and have reason to anticipate rejection if they try to set up house in the better areas of a city. The way in which our own West Indian immigrants have tended to concentrate in the more deteriorated neighbourhoods is an illustration of this. Thus the community life of the old settled area breaks down. With change and mobility to be seen on all sides, people neither know each other, nor care very much about each other. There is little shared community feeling and no sense of values held in common. People do not know what is expected of them in the way of behaviour, and have no feeling that, whatever they do, anybody will mind or even notice. It is small wonder, in these circumstances, if their behaviour does run to extremes, and that it leads, often enough, to delinquency.

Emotional isolation may also have its bearing on the situation. Lonely children often strike out, as a first clumsy attempt to relate to, or be noticed by others. Residents of a slum area with a highly mobile population can register through a court appearance (to their own satisfaction at least) the fact that they are members of a community : that who they are and what they do does matter to someone, even if it is only the police. Perhaps the most striking analogy of all to this situation is to be found in the behaviour of the deprived child. Unable to obtain the parental love he needs, he misbehaves in order to attract, at the very least, punitive attention on the part of adults.

The semi-detached council house, in its tree-lined street, may seem to have very little in common with the damp, gloomy, and dilapidated hovels in the terraces or around the courtyards of a slum area. But on the view now being examined, it is not, as we have seen, the physical side of the community which is to be emphasized, but its psychological side. Seen from this point of view, the two kinds of neighbourhood have much in common. Removal to a new estate breaks many precious neighbourhood and kinship ties; many young housewives, more dependent upon neighbourhood contact for their social satisfactions than their husbands who go out to work during the day, become very lonely, and take a long time to settle down. They still think of themselves as having their roots in the area from which they came, and some of them eventually return there if they can. The others go back as often as they can, to see 'Mum', to gossip with the neighbours, and buy their groceries at the corner shop. As a number of surveys have shown in recent years, the wider kinship group of grandmother, her daughters, and all their families has a great deal of significance in lower working-class life, and the breaking up of this 'family', when it occurs through removal to a new estate, has been experienced by everybody concerned as a major disaster.

But there is at least a future for the new estate; a slum area has only final destruction before it. And as time passes, and personal relationships develop over the garden fences of the housing estate, a sense of community begins to develop. It often manifests itself at first in ways which are by no means welcome to the authorities; the rent-strike, for instance, is not an uncommon feature of this phase in a community's development. Once again illumination is to be found in comparing adult behaviour with that of young children, who can find fewer plausible excuses for their behaviour and therefore display the psychological element in its undiluted form. They have no qualms about uniting, at the earliest stage in their social development in the common persecution of some unfortunate child, who for some reason or other is a convenient target. The estate dwellers may have real grievances about their rent (or about education, or about the lack of shops, or a pub, or whatever it may be), but to admit this is in no way to explain the alacrity with which formerly suspicious and isolated neighbours will join together in a militant campaign of this kind, if the opportunity arises at the right stage in the community's progress towards maturity. One cannot help but feel that a condition for loving each other is that they should sometimes have somebody whom they can join together in hating.

But if the first stage may be one of rebellion, it is eventually succeeded, in most cases, by steady growth in staid respectability. For present purposes, what matters most is that delinquency usually falls fairly steeply at this time. In Leicester, an estate which fifteen years ago had the highest delinquency rate in the city, has a rate now which is just the same as that of the most respectable middle-class neighbourhood. Even more significantly, the only estate of long standing in which the delinquency rate has not fallen is one in which, for special reasons, the rate of residential mobility has continued high.

This, then, is one view about the origin of the delinquency area : that it is the symptom of a sickness in the local community, a degree of immaturity in the inter-personal life of the neighbourhood. If this is the case, we must look for relief to measures designed to bring about more speedy development in new communities. But this development has to be the result of spontaneous activity by the community itself. The degree of cohesion which develops around such issues as a rent strike shows that if a new community can be helped to recognize its common interests, its collective motivation will be stirred; but they have to be genuine indigenous interests of its own and not interests which well-meaning and possibly rather self-righteous outsiders think they ought to have.

Meanwhile there are other rival explanations in the field, which, although they differ in detail among themselves, do have a certain core of ideas in common. They deny, first of all, that there is any serious disorganization in the local community life, which they see instead as a highly effective agency of social training. Social disintegration is present, but as a characteristic of the wider society of which the local neighbourhood forms only a part. Because of divisions in the great society, individuals brought up within, and adjusted to, the local way of life, become for that very reason ill-adjusted to the way of life of the rest of the country, and often, as a result, delinquent.

From the point of view of the law-abiding citizen, the dissident behaviour of residents of delinquency areas seems antisocial and immoral enough. Surveys of social attitudes in areas of this kind suggest that it has hardly the same connotation in their minds. They tend, as do most of us, to think of their own ways as normal and desirable. To get this into perspective, it is only necessary to bear in mind the use of the word 'win' in the Army to refer to kinds of stealing which soldiers accept as legitimate; or the distinction in industry, referred to above, between pilfering and stealing. Because their behaviour clashes with ours is no proof in itself that they are wrong.

Consider, for example, the case of Ben. In the tenements in which he lived, people had scant respect for rights of property. If given too much change by a shop assistant they would be unlikely to give it back; they would probably look upon a person who did as 'a bit of mug'. And Ben could never understand why anyone should want to bother too much about the future. For instance, he could never see any point in saving. If you asked him why, the essential burden of his answer would have been : why do without, in the interests of an ever-receding tomorrow, when life is here waiting to be enjoyed?

But though, in all these respects, Ben's standards may have been different from those which are approved of in respectable society, he did not see them as in any sense worse or lower. They were the standards he had grown up with, and to him they were good standards and natural ones. As an illustration one might take the attitude to children in Ben's locality. The foreigners from more respectable areas might describe these children as neglected and running wild, but their parents, Ben's neighbours, would speak instead of giving the children freedom to enjoy themselves, and would have little understanding or sympathy for the genteel restrictions laid on children in middle- and upper working-class families.

According to the choice of phrase, Ben had himself 'run wild' or 'enjoyed himself'. As long as he could remember, he had run with a gang, which used to meet around a street lamp after supper, laughing and fooling, and planning adventures. Ben was always there, for he was very sociable. In this, also, he reflected the standards of the community which had nurtured him, for he, and those among whom he lived, are nothing if not neighbourly. They are interested (often inquisitively so) in each other's affairs; but it is a warm interest which leads also to much mutual help and support between neighbours. If one contrasts this with the aloof and rather self-centred attitude which often masquerades as a belief in privacy among the more respectable, it must be apparent that there is something to be said for the way of life of Ben and his neighbours.

Ben's gang, then, in key with the culture within which they had been raised, were gregarious and impatient for satisfaction, and had no real respect for either authority or other people's property. Set boys like these in a decaying and congested area, where there are few things that active children can do without trespassing or breaking some law or other, and very soon law-breaking becomes a game in its own right, bringing with it all the excitement of competition, and the extra spice of mild danger. Ben was a bright lad and learned quickly; he became adept at many kinds of mischief. When the gang wanted to break into some interesting building, a warehouse perhaps, he would lead the way. It was on one such foray that he first fell into the hands of the police. This meant a year's probation for him but it did him no harm with his gang. It was a kind of official seal on the predatory ability he had already displayed in practice, and he became the unchallenged leader of his gang from then on.

He was bound to be caught again, and this time it meant a spell in an approved school. Here new vistas were opened up to him. To many of the boys with whom he now lived and worked in the reformatory, his record of misdemeanours was very small beer. They belonged, as they so often told him, to the world of 'real crime'; they knew its personalities, they knew something of the opportunities it offered, and above all they knew that success as a criminal required more than intelligence and daring, for there was an apprenticeship to be served, skilled and highly specialized crafts to be learned. The excitement of it all, the promise it held of opportunities which would otherwise be beyond his hopes, caught his imagination. And his gregarious nature led him to seek the status in the school that only membership of this more delinquent *élite* could give him.

When Ben emerged from the school, he not only talked like a professional criminal but thought like one. Instead of returning home, he took up some of the criminal contacts he had been able to make, and eventually apprenticed himself to a master safe cracksman. He learned all he could from this man, and then set up in business on his own account. As a 'peterman' (a safeblower), he is proud of his skill, and has acquired much prestige. He found his friends and his wife from among criminals; and as befits a successful and conservative professional man he takes no unnecessary risks. Although he has been twice in prison, his attitude here is rather like that of the miner towards accidents: he rarely thinks about the danger of being caught, and when he does he is fatalistic about it.

Without doubt, some offenders are abnormal individuals, and an attempt will be made in the chapters which follow to try to understand some of the abnormalities involved. It could hardly be asserted, however, that Ben is abnormal. He is neither neurotic nor insane, he loves his children and his wife, and cleans his car on Sunday mornings. He has many friends, in the same line of business as himself. He is proud of his craftsmanship and his success. Nor could it be argued that he is antisocial, in any literal sense. He has always been very obedient to the conventions and public opinion of his own social world, and if he had been less so, might also have been less likely to end up as a confirmed adult criminal.

One possible implication here is that what we are inclined to think of as a national way of life and system of morality is no more than the socially dominant point of view – dominant either because it is the view of a majority, or of a group, like the middle class who have the education and the economic and political power to enforce their own set of values upon the country as a whole. Some American sociologists have argued that American society is dominated by middle-class standards in this way. To succeed, and thus to earn the respect of your fellows, you have to satisfy the middle-class criterion of material success. The unsuccessful man is a failure, and of no account. One might well feel that the lack of material success is its own punishment, but under this austere creed you lose also your status in the community.

This places many of the more underprivileged sections of the population in an intolerable position. Their lack of education, of capital, and of useful social contacts puts them so far back in the race for achievement that the scales are heavily weighted against them from the beginning. And yet they are told, in effect, that unless they are successful, there is, for them, no niche worth having in respectable society. If this is a correct description of their dilemma, it is hardly surprising if they reject the middle-class culture which treats them so cruelly. According to Cohen, the destructive gang-delinquency, common among teenagers in the poorer areas, is a deliberately aggressive way of rejecting an official community which has no place for them. Other young people being more interested in acceptance within their own subculture, and prevented, by lack of advantage and a host of middle-class restrictions, from achieving the success (mainly financial) which would assure their position even there, see nothing wrong in subverting institutions and laws of what they feel to be little more than an unjust despotism. Prevented unfairly, as they feel, by the law from achieving their legitimate ends legally, they set out to achieve them anyway, even if it means breaking the law.

Long experience of this kind of situation is said to engender general attitudes towards the law and towards other sections of the national community which are deeply rooted, and eventually passed on from generation to generation through the normal processes of social training. Children learn these attitudes within their families, as part of their picture of the world around them : this is what people are like, this is what society is like, and this is how the normal person in our neighbourhood is expected to behave. Delinquent patterns are thus created by conflicts in the great society, and perpetuated because of the effectiveness of a process of socialization which one would rather have expected to lead to satisfactory social adjustment. Social adjustment is, in fact, satisfactory within the local community; it is the integration of that community within the national life which is at fault.

It is not easy to choose between these two competing theories about the origins of what is becoming known as subcultural criminality. Perhaps one does not have to. Perhaps community disorganization and inter-cultural conflict both have their roots in the same soil – that of emotional deprivation. The deprivation of inter-personal satisfactions is apparent enough in the case of the estate-dweller. The thirst for status emphasized in the other approach also points to a need for acceptance and recognition by other people. Indeed, the status factor (as will be shown later) may, in its own right, be a weaker element in the situation than even this would imply.

Studies by Spinley, Kerr, and others, of differences in family structure as between different social classes in this country indicate that lower working-class children are often more deprived of maternal love than their middle-class counterparts. The baby is always made much of, petted, dressed-up, and shown off. But as families are large, a child is soon displaced from this favoured position by a younger rival, who also then proceeds, for a very brief spell, to monopolize all the attention of his mother. Each child in turn, without the preliminary 'hardening off' through social training, which a middle-class child would have received, is dispatched to the company of his brothers and sisters, and so becomes very dependent upon them for acceptance and love. It may be that it is out of this situation that the extreme sociability of the 'rough' working-class person is derived.

This sudden and almost brutal separation from his mother seems likely to have its effect also upon a child's sense of values. Immediate gratifications are sought, because 'who knows what will happen tomorrow?' The good things of life may be snatched away at any time, and without any warning. And those gratifications must be tangible, not elusive and disappointing personal relationships: a limitation which leads to an almost obsessive preoccupation with these basically unsatisfying substitutes. How, also, does one cope within oneself with so sudden a demand for independence and maturity? The middle-class child is allowed to grow up gradually, to set about controlling and restraining his infantile urges one by one, as he feels strong enough, and as he is able to weaken their hold on him by finding alternative satisfactions: meanwhile his mother's love and support sustain him. The rough working-class child has none of these advantages, but is flung in at the deep end. Anger and resentment are likely consequences; but he seems also to grow up with what is often inaccurately called a 'weak character', i.e. weak inner controls, because he has been given no time or opportunity to develop anything stronger. Impulsive behaviour, often destructive and hostile, and almost infantile in character, results from such deficiencies in the ego. He is under constant inner stress, as weak inhibitions and restraints seek to maintain their tenuous control over powerful and unintegrated instincts – and often fail to do so.

It is widely accepted by psychologists that the individual's moral judgement arises out of the close emotional bond between an infant and his parents in a small family. Where such a bond does not exist, conscience can hardly develop. Various observers have noted that the rough working class do not have a very strong sense of guilt, being more sensitive to ridicule than to an appeal to abstract morality. They are, in other words, well adapted to the kind of group situation in which they live much of their lives. They are controlled by public opinion, and not by the 'still, small voice'; a state of affairs which is very appropriate to a way of life in which, as in the case of Ben and his neighbours, so much is public. A personal censor is more necessary in middle-class circles, where real privacy does exist.

The early family experience of the rough working-class individual is enough to account for his characteristic behaviour and for his proneness to delinquency. And the very difference between his behaviour and that of other groups, the clashes which his impatient and violently unstable nature brings about as he makes contact with those less driven, are more than enough to bring about class antagonisms of the kind noted by writers like Cohen. Suppose that a group so conditioned to dependence upon their fellows are then robbed even of this support. This is what the decay of community life in a slum, or its immaturity in a new housing estate, seems to imply. Are not existing aggressions, the demand for material compensations, the inability to tolerate frustration, going to be greatly augmented, leading to an increase in behaviour which the rest of the community calls delinquency?

This analysis is couched, of course, in the language of the middle class. The rough working class are seen as 'deprived' and 'unstable', as in some serious way marred by a sub-standard upbringing. It cannot be too frequently repeated that this is a partial and culturally biased viewpoint. We cannot easily observe our fellows apart from the distortions imposed by our own upbringing, and this may prevent us from seeing the more positive values implicit in another way of life. Nor should words like 'immoral' and 'abnormal' be lightly used in such a context. In a 'rough' neighbourhood it would be the middle-class person who would seem abnormal, and undoubtedly (if he stayed) would feel sufficiently an 'odd man out' to want to try to change his behaviour. But what really matters is that a permanently dissentient minority (whether in the right or not), has grown up as a threat, not only to our property and peace of mind, but perhaps to the solidarity of our national life. There is much talk about Western countries being divided into two nations (the poor and the rich), or two cultures (scientists and nonscientists), but here is a schism between social classes which is less often recognized, but which may have even more serious implications for the future than any of the others.

Seen in this light, delinquent attitudes rooted in persisting inter-cultural conflict may, after all, be symptoms of a graver disease than that of social disorganization alone. Given time and recognition of the problem, we may confidently expect that disorganized new communities will settle down, so long as there are no deeply ingrained social attitudes in the way of this. If the process of social maturation were too slow, chronic sub-cultural delinquency might result, but it would be a superficial manifestation, no longer fed by any underlying malaise. The alternative source of delinquent behaviour is, however, itself a serious social disease. We must not complain if so serious a division in our national life is reflected in differing attitudes about desirable forms of social behaviour. Our society may at times seem in danger of being torn apart by the conflict between the law-abiding and the law-breakers, but if there is anything in the view expounded here, it is already divided enough; the persistence of subcultural criminality is no more than an external registration of that fact.

Chapter 3

Born Criminals?

Some of us may attempt to deny our own implication with the crime problem by blaming it all upon the residents of the delinquency areas, 'Them', the disreputable slum dwellers, or the spendthrift residents of council houses. Another even commoner way of putting ourselves in the right is to say that crime is 'in the blood'. Somebody we know gets into trouble and at once people remember that his father was once in trouble with the police when he was a boy, or that there was a cousin who went bankrupt, an aunt who was divorced, or a grandfather who got merrily drunk from time to time.

Evidence of this kind is so flimsy that we could obviously only be brought to believe in it if our own emotions and needs were strongly involved. Reason will be given for suggesting that they are; it is our very similarity to the criminal which we are trying to deny by portraying him as essentially someone from another world – or at least another family.

But if the examples we give in everyday conversation of the way in which abnormality or crime runs in families are highly suspect, there are not lacking some better-authenticated accounts of the so-called degenerate families, which have been offered as proof of the view that antisocial behaviour is 'in the blood'. A series of studies like this appeared in the United States before the First World War. The family trees of the Jukeses, the Kallikaks, and the Nams, were worked out over long periods of time, and an attempt made to determine how many criminals, paupers, prostitutes, mental defectives, etc., they produced. Often these figures seemed rather startling at first sight: of 709 Jukeses traced, there were 140 criminals, seven being murderers. At the other extreme was the family of Jonathan

Edwards, which included no criminals but many distinguished American citizens, some of whom reached the highest positions in the land. It would, of course, not be surprising if the criminality of the Jukeses and the Kallikaks was exaggerated. If people want to see the explanation of crime in familial incidence, they will look for it there. The old saying about 'giving a dog a bad name' has a lot of truth in it also. It is particularly important to note that the apparently high proportion of criminal Jukeses is, according to the most recent figures, less than the proportion of the general population who have probably committed an offence at some time or other in their lives. Jonathan Edwards, also, may have had no criminal descendants, but he had criminal ancestors.

More scientific studies of this question, from Cyril Burt in 1923 onwards, do show that there is a tendency for criminality to run in families, but this by no means proves that there is an inherited element in it. As the American criminologists Sutherland and Cressey point out, 'The use of the fork in eating has been a trait of many families for several generations, but this does not prove that a tendency to use a fork is inherited'. To what extent the problem may be blamed upon heredity and to what extent upon social training within the family, possibly during the very earliest and most malleable years, must be determined by some other means.

The most interesting of these more direct approaches to the problem has been the study of identical twins. In order to make this method clear, a preliminary word is necessary upon the biological process by which twins are conceived. In most cases, when an ovum (or egg cell) in the female has been fertilized by the male sperm, the cell begins to divide, forming at first a pair of cells, and eventually, after successive divisions, a cluster. It is by such a process that the full-grown organism is eventually built up. Microscopic observation has shown that when the first division takes place, the chromosomes which carry the hereditary traits are split down the middle, one half of each chromosome going to the left into one of the subdivisions, and the other half to the right into the other. Thus it can be assumed that the inherited potential of each subdivision is identical.

Sometimes, however, instead of continuing together as part of the same organism, the two newly created cells separate and begin to develop independently. In such circumstances, we have twins. And just as the innate endowment of the two cells would have been identical if they had continued together, so we may assume that the inheritance of the twins is quite literally identical. In contrast, non-identical twins are bound to be much less similar in heredity. They develop from ova which were separate from the beginning, but happen to have been fertilized at about the same time.

There are some obvious similarities between identical twins. For instance, they are very similar in appearance. It has been argued that if they could be shown, also, to be strikingly similar with regard to their criminal behaviour, one would be as justified in attributing this to heredity as, for example, their similar appearance. The pioneer in this kind of approach was a German scientist, Johannes Lange. He compared thirteen pairs of identical and seventeen pairs of non-identical twins where one of each pair had served a prison sentence, and found that in over three quarters of the identical twins, but in less than one in eight of the non-identical, the other twin also had been in prison.

But what Lange, and the other researchers who followed his lead failed to recognize was that results of this kind pointed to a hereditary cause for criminality only if one assumed that environment had nothing to do with it. In fact, there is every reason to believe that environment has a good deal to do with the differences which Lange and the others found. We all know how difficult it is to distinguish identical twins from each other, and if most people continually mistake them for each other their social experience is likely to become very similar – much more so than that of non-identical twins, who are easily told apart. It is also generally agreed that twins are very attached to each other, and have similar interests, drawing them into ways of life which are either shared or very much alike. On the strength of this, one might be tempted to assume a position completely contradictory to that of Lange, and say that the more similar criminal records of identical twins, as compared with their non-identical counterparts, are readily explained by their more similar environmental experience. Just as Lange, however, took the irrelevance of the environment for granted, so much an extreme environmental position fails to deal at all with the possibility that inheritance has something to do with the problem.

Lombroso, the great Italian criminologist, who many see as the founder of the modern scientific study of crime, believed, like Lange, that criminality was mainly inborn, arguing that the possession of certain physical characteristics (presumably themselves innate) went with criminal tendencies. When the popular 'Whodunit' describes the criminal who figures in its pages as low-browed, having small, restless, or alternatively cold, glassy eyes, and fleshy, protruding lips, it is bearing witness almost in Lombroso's own words to the influence which his ideas had for a time upon thinking about criminals.

His imagination was fired when, as a doctor, he carried out a post-mortem examination on a notorious bandit, Vilella, who had died in prison. He was very struck by the similarities between certain unusual features of Vilella's skull, and those found in the lower animals.

This was not merely an idea but a revelation. At the sight of that skull, I seemed to see all of a sudden, lighted up as a vast plain under a flaming sky, the problems of the nature of the criminal – an atavistic being who reproduces in his person the ferocious instincts of primitive humanity and the inferior animals. Thus were explained anatomically the enormous jaws, high cheek bones, prominent superciliary arches, solitary lines in the palms, extreme size of the orbits, handle-shaped or sessile ears found in criminals, savages, and apes, insensibility to pain, extremely acute sight, tattooing, excessive idleness, love of orgies, and the irresistible craving for evil for its own sake, the desire not only to extinguish life in the victim, but to mutilate the corpse, tear its flesh and drink its blood.

Whatever criticisms may subsequently have been made about Lombroso, it could not be claimed that he was not enthusiastic, but his researches were carried out with too little regard for the safeguards of scientific method for much reliance to be placed upon his conclusions. His refutation in 1913, thirty-seven years after his famous book *L'Uomo Delinquente* first appeared, was effected by Charles Goring, an English prison doctor, who carried out a careful scientific study of English convicts, and concluded that the physical stigmata of criminality, upon which Lombroso relied so much, were a myth.

At first Lombroso saw criminal behaviour, and the physical stigmata, as 'throw-backs' to an earlier evolutionary type, one of man's animal ancestors. Later on he paid more attention to the idea of degeneration, or tainted inheritance. Neither of these views any longer carry much weight among scientists. Charles Goring made it impossible any longer to believe in the idea of a criminal whose degraded nature is, as with Dorian Gray, revealed to a horrified world by his villainous appearance. Research on a possible relationship between physique and criminality had to take a new turn. This has proved very fruitful indeed, giving a new slant to the argument about innate or hereditary elements in behaviour.

It is based upon the finding of Kretschmer and others, that certain kinds of temperament seemed to be associated with certain kinds of general physical conformation. On the one hand there is the plump, short individual: he is the warm-hearted extrovert, a hail-fellow-well-met, life-and-soul-of-the-party type of person. In striking contrast to him is the tall, thin, and angular person, who is said to be of an inturned, dreamy, or meditative bent. Finally, there is the strongly-muscled, powerful individual, who is temperamentally thrusting and vigorous.

None of the more moderate supporters of this view suggests for a minute that one's personality is predetermined according to one's physical conformation. Temperament is no more than the emotional basis upon which personality is built. But it does set limits to the kind of development which the experiences of life can bring about in the individual. Although each mature personality is unique just as the experiences which have created it are unique, broad similarities in temperament between different people can exist and remain recognizable throughout life. In more recent work along these lines by Sheldon it is also denied that there is a simple three-fold classification of this kind within which everybody can be grouped. All these physical and temperamental types are seen rather as characteristics which we can all possess in different degrees and in a variety of combinations. Which particular combination of temperamental traits we happen to possess will be revealed by the particular combination of physical traits we display.

The relevance of all this to the problem of crime follows from investigations carried out by the most famous of the American criminologists, Professor and Mrs Glueck. These investigations seem to show that the possession of certain combinations of physico-temperamental traits goes with a tendency to certain kinds of delinquent behaviour, or even with a greater or lesser proneness to delinquency in general.

This is a highly sophisticated theory. There is no crude assumption, here, that criminal tendencies, in themselves, are inborn or inherited. What is suggested is that temperament, going with physique, is inherited, and that this affects one's response to the stimuli and stresses of life, so that, in certain circumstances, one may as a result become a criminal. It sees temperament as one factor in the creation of a criminal – a partner with the environment. In explaining how, as their researches suggest, the more thrusting individuals, with their more powerful, mesomorphic physique, come to be more prone to criminality than those in whom other traits predominate, the Gluecks say:

> In the exciting, stimulating, but little-controlled and culturally inconsistent environment of the under-privileged area, such boys readily give expression to their untamed impulses and their self-centred desires by means of various forms of delinquent behaviour.

But they do not put all the blame on the thrusting mesomorph. Though his is the most delinquency-prone type, their work showed no less clearly in what circumstances other temperament types may become implicated.

It is to temperament, therefore, rather than, for example, to intelligence that we must look for the innate contribution to our crime problem. There is no 'inborn' correlation between criminal behaviour and low intelligence. The acts of delinquents seem rather stupid; they continue with their misbehaviour, often in spite of its unprofitableness to them, in spite of frequent punishment, and the very low standard of life which crime entails for most of its practitioners. There are professional criminals who make a success of their careers, but many do spend years in prison and make very little money to compensate them for the risk, and the ingenuity and industry which they have to display in order to carry through 'a job'. If one evaluates their behaviour in a rational way, it is apt to seem very unintelligent.

Yet it is clear that not all criminals are unintelligent, and that many need to be highly intelligent in order even to attempt the kinds of crime which they commit. If the burglar is to have any chance at all of succeeding, he must be able to organize his operations in detail, and with great efficiency. He must be able to collect together a team of experts, and keep them working together as a team until they are all well away. And then he has to dispose of the loot at a good price. In their different ways, the criminals who specialize in fraud or false pretences must be not only personally prepossessing, but also have fluent tongues and agile minds. Only the simpler and more impulsive crimes are available to the person of low intelligence, and even at these he will probably be unsuccessful.

When we come to the conclusion that criminals must be rather stupid to behave in the way they do, it is because we are assuming that in stealing, for instance, their motive is the most obvious one, the idea of making a quick and easy profit. But if one knew them better, one might come to recognize the more personal needs which their criminality satisfies. For Ben, described earlier, criminality satisfied a need for status and acceptance in the social world within which he lived – a world which was more real to him as a source of satisfaction than the law-abiding world surrounding it. For others, it might be even more intimate psychological needs (still to be discussed) which are being satisfied, often in a curious, symbolical way, by stealing, violence, or the like. By some criteria, crime may seem unintelligent, but by others it is highly purposive, achieving very well the objectives which the criminal has set himself.

Recent studies confirm this view that, although low (or high) intelligence may be a factor in particular cases, on the whole criminals are not very different in this respect from the rest of the population. This is very much a modern view : a few years ago the contrary was taken for granted. We have always tended to over-value intelligence in this country. Parents whose children fail in the 11-plus are often not merely disappointed, but positively ashamed of their offspring for this. The ready association of criminality with low intelligence seems to be merely another example of our belief that intelligence is almost in itself a virtue, and stupidity a kind of vice. Perhaps we are at last beginning, however, to recognize that there are other sides to human personality, some of them, like love and tolerance, being as useful socially, and possibly of higher moral worth. The highly intelligent criminal is, after all, just so much the more dangerous on that account.

The classical Lombrosian view was a very fatalistic one, and some of the early statements of the physico-temperament school seemed also to imply that the inborn predisposition in the criminal was so strong that not much could be done for him. Sheldon argued quite frankly for controlled breeding, but such a cure may be worse than the disease. Even if it were the only solution, many would feel that to interfere, in this way, with people's individual rights raised issues which went far beyond the limits of our crime problem.

Fortunately, as must now be fairly clear, this is by no means the only, or even the easiest approach to the crime problem. There may be a constitutional element at work, but other factors are also present. Temperament is only the foundation; the superstructure of personality has still to be created by a process of interaction with other people, in which our emotions are aroused, relationship of affection or hostility established, general attitudes acquired – a psychological process in which so much detail has to be filled in that the foundation itself eventually comes to look quite different. This has occasionally been well illustrated by twin studies in cases in which one of the pair was and the other was not a criminal. Even in adult life such twins show striking resemblances in traits which are known to be predominantly innate. When tested with the electro-encephalogram, they are found to have remarkably similar patterns of electrical activity in the brain. Their intelligence quotients tend to be very much alike. But in personality they diverge widely, the criminal being more in conflict within himself than his non-criminal twin. Neurotic conflicts of this kind are known to arise mainly as a result of the experiences a child has within the family during his early years, and even twins can be treated differently from each other by their parents.

Not only is temperament merely a starting point, but what happens to the individual afterwards may determine what it is the starting point to. In itself it may not even initiate a predisposition to crime. The mesomorphic individual, according to his subsequent experience, may perhaps become a criminal, stigmatized as antisocial, on the one hand, or an aggressively successful but socially esteemed business man on the other. Moreover, temperament, as the Gluecks have shown, responds to environmental stimulus : the mesomorphic, thrusting youth kicks against the pricks of a restrictive social setting.

There remains nevertheless the possibility that innate temperamental trends may in themselves be such as to limit the amount of modification which can occur in them – a sort of built-in self-defeating mechanism. Such could be the case for example if an individual were born with a defect in his ability to make social relationships. If the further development of our social nature takes place, as already suggested, largely through our interactions with other people, a person who was constitutionally crippled in this way would be precluded from benefiting from social intercourse, and so prevented from maturing into sociality through it. The defect in social capacity could thus be self-perpetuating. He would remain unrelated to, and very largely uncognizant of the currents of social life around him; and this though not inevitably leading to crime is bound to mean that he becomes a chronic misfit, an isolated oddity. Similarly it is sometimes argued that a congenital inability to develop a moral sense, or to generalize from experience and therefore benefit from it, marks out the constitutional social misfit from the rest of us.

It is on grounds such as these that the incorrigible criminal (the psychopathic criminal as he is often called in the clinical literature) is still sometimes described as a 'born criminal'. But this conclusion does not necessarily follow. The psychopathic personality, displaying the three main features of psychopathy described above (criminality, asociality, amorality) is often found in a mental hospital after an episode of bizarre behaviour, or in prison after committing a crime. And reasons will be given in the next chapter for believing that his particular personality defects have developed as a result of early experience within the family, rather than from 'flaws in the genes'. For the contrary view there is, in contrast, little firm evidence of any kind.

A danger in talking about crime is always that of oversimplifying the problem. As we have seen, it is only too easy to oversimplify trends in criminality; criminal statistics are complicated and can be highly misleading. In the same way it is only too easy to oversimplify and exaggerate the contribution made by the inborn constitution. The evidence suggests that it is unlikely to be decisive in the making of a criminal. So many subsequent and very formative experiences have also to make themselves felt in his life.

It is really rather astonishing that the alternative view could ever have been held. What is crime, after all, does depend upon what laws happen to be passed; the idea of a born criminal would imply an innate tendency to break particular laws; like those protecting private property or proscribing homosexual relationships. How disconcerting then to find oneself born into a community like that of the Eskimoes, or certain Melanesian peoples, who are not much interested in property rights; or to make one's entrée in a bedroom in Scandinavia where homosexuality is tolerated, or in the Long House of certain Indian tribes among whom it is not only tolerated, but is a recognized mode of adjustment to society. Just as social processes have to be set in motion in order to make particular acts into crimes, so a social contribution (either of the early psychologically predisposing kind referred to above or of a later stimuli-stress variety) is necessary to change an organism with a certain kind of biological predisposition into a person with a particular kind of social predisposition.

Chapter 4

The Disinherited

Modern ideas about physiological and inborn elements in criminality may bear only the slightest family resemblance to the cruder ideas of Lombroso. In one other respect at least, however, his contribution to modern thinking has been much more directly important. He it was, more than anyone else, who signalized the change from a moralistic to a scientific attitude towards crime : that crime is brought about by causal factors – rather than by some kind of moral defect in the individual offender. Lombroso saw these causes to lie in the innate constitution of the individual. We have seen this to be unsatisfactory as a complete explanation of criminality. The more moderate view however, that what matters is the innate potentiality as shaped by subsequent experience, absolves the criminal from personal responsibility just as completely. Something has already been said in Chapter 2 about factors impinging upon the individual from the wider environment; the present discussion will be focused upon experiences arising within the family circle during the formative years of infancy. We are now concerned with psychological development rather than with social pressures.

Most psychologists who study crime nowadays look for its causes in mental factors which lie outside the individual's control, and no one did more to encourage this than Sigmund Freud, the founder of psycho-analysis. Freud was a thoroughgoing believer in what he called 'psychic determinism'. Everything that we do, he contended, has a discoverable cause in the shape of a personal conflict or anxiety. This applies even to the most trivial of human acts such as slips of the tongue or the inability to remember a particular name. The slip of the tongue reveals an underlying motive, conflicting with that which the words, spoken correctly, would have expressed. The name which is continually forgotten has associations for us which we would rather forget. Crime too has its origin in our personal emotional lives. And it is by our early family experience that our personalities have been shaped.

Such a view is less fatalistic than that of Lombroso. Something, after all, can be done about changing methods of child-rearing; and although the early years are seen by the psycho-analyst as of overwhelming importance, he does not leave out of account the possibility of some limited changes in psychological make-up in later years. Psycho-analytical treatment is a process which is intended to bring about just such changes. But if less fatalistic, the psycho-analytical approach makes many more demands upon us than does Lombrosianism. The offender may be absolved, but great responsibility is placed upon the shoulders of parents. What their child becomes later in life, whether criminal, carpenter, or cabinet minister, is seen to be largely the result of their attitudes and behaviour.

Psycho-analysts and clinical psychologists in general see the young child as a young animal, possessed of powerful biological needs. He seeks gratification for these instincts at all costs, and at this stage in his development has little regard for the needs or wishes of other people. We expect such behaviour of young infants, but if he goes on to adult life without moderating his demands and egotistical attitude, he will be a very antisocial person, and possibly a very dangerous one. What is normal in the child, may be abnormal and criminal in the adult. Everything therefore depends on the process of socialization which takes place within the family. Although families differ widely, most parents are sufficiently imbued with the standards of their own society to want to transmit them to their children. If they belong to nonconformist subcultures, like those found in the delinquency areas already described, then the standards they will instil in their children will be those of their own deviant group; this is possibly the most potent of the factors making for the persistence of delinquent subcultures. But for the vast majority, the family is a positive socializing force.

Difficulties are more likely to arise when the structure or functioning of the family is impaired in some way, so that, like a broken wire in an electrical circuit, it cannot carry its 'charge' or quota of social training. August Aichhorn, the great Austrian pioneer in the treatment of delinquent boys, argued that children gave up their instinctual demands only in exchange for love. If they received love without any corresponding demand for a renunciation of their more primitive wishes, or more commonly, if they received no love at all, then they continued to be the same instinct-driven persons throughout life. A child in the more normal family, which both gives love and exacts conformity, gradually acquires inner controls by which he sets limits upon his own behaviour, but this process has its own hazards. Parents can be too censorious, especially if they are rather neurotic – afraid of and therefore hostile to their own personal drives. It is not easy for the child, whose instinctual needs are so urgent, to get them in hand quickly, and if too much is expected of him by his parents, one possibility is that he will incorporate within himself a highly repressive and frustrating set of inner controls. He becomes well-behaved, perhaps too much so, but at the cost of great inner conflict. The distinction here, says Aichhorn, is between the delinquent, whose instincts are not restrained in any way and who is therefore in constant conflict with his environment, and the neurotic who is in conflict within himself.

These ideas have been elaborated and scientifically tested by subsequent writers (notably John Bowlby) but remain essentially as Aichhorn formulated them, as possibly the most important single contribution to the psychology of crime. Thus, the only major change in recent years has been the emphasis placed by Bowlby upon a break in the mother-infant relationship as a result of the child's being physically removed from his mother's care. Through such complete separation, the child is deprived of love, and, as a result, of the social heritage which is transmitted through its agency. In consequence he remains a strange creature, dominated by his impulses, with apparently no sense of guilt, and with such a deficiency in his sense of reality that he can do the most bizarre or the most dangerous things without apparently realizing their incongruity. Neither punishment nor blame seems to affect him very much, and he lives in an isolated world, in which other people seem to have little meaning or importance for him. He shows no sign of wanting either the company or the friendship of other people, and has no sympathy or feeling for them.

A man like this, let loose in the world without having been trained for it, is bound to create havoc wherever he goes. George Smith eventually tried to strangle a woman in a dark entry. He did not look like a strangler; his appearance was mild enough, and when dragged off his intended victim he was quite cool and matter-of-fact. Nor did he show any emotion when he admitted that he had tried to kill her, 'because I wanted her necklace for my girl'. It was hardly credible that a string of almost worthless glass beads, casually glimpsed on a woman's neck in a pub, could lead a man to attempt murder; and indeed, George's own motivation did not seem to be very powerful. He did not, in fact, seem to want the beads very much.

Such behaviour seems hardly sane, and yet there was no doubt that George was sane in the ordinary sense of the word. He knew what he had been trying to do, and could talk quite rationally about it. Nevertheless, the court ordered a psychiatric investigation, and in the course of this, still odder facts about him came to light. His teacher, an old man now retired, remembered him, and the strange things he did, very well. He talked of finding George leaning a long ladder against the glass of the big window in a third floor classroom, about to climb up it to see over the wall of the factory building next door, and failing to realize that the window would have broken and thrown him down three storeys to the school yard. At another time he played for weeks in a barn on a local farm without anybody knowing. He made tunnels through the hay and used to crawl through them like a mole. But eventually he decided that dark tunnels were not so very much fun; he built a cave in the heart of the hay-pile – and took a lighted candle in with him, so that he could see around! Inevitably the hay caught fire, and the barn and its contents were completely destroyed. It was only the prompt arrival of the fire-brigade which saved the farmhouse itself, but George escaped with singed hair and eyebrows.

This exploit brought him at last to the notice of the police, and he was sent away to an approved school. Never since has he been out of custody for very long. While in one correctional institution or another, he has been too closely supervised to get into much trouble; but no one knew what he might not do during his brief periods of freedom. And whether free or confined, a thread of irresponsibility ran through all his behaviour. It was as if he lived in a different world of space and time from the rest of us. For him, for instance, the laws of cause and effect might never have existed: he never recognized the consequences of his actions to be consequences, and threatening situations were never seen as such. If questioned about some misdemeanour he would admit it quite readily but with a complete lack of any sense of guilt, or even of concern about what might be done to him in return. Nor did either remonstrance or punishment make the slightest difference to him. One reformatory head, who had tried to reason with him, said, 'He'd listen to you politely enough, and even make appropriate responses. But you never felt any of it was really going in. In fact you hardly felt that you were in contact with him at all – it was as if somebody had cut the telephone wire.'

As the psychiatric inquiry proceeded, this lack of contact with people emerged as one of George's most striking characteristics. As a child he did not seem to care whether he played with other children or not. He would, if they happened to be around, but it seemed to make very little difference to him whether they were around or not. One witness after another spoke of the curious feeling of detachment which he communicated. 'It was as if he were behind a glass case,' said one. Another, almost echoing the approved school headmaster, said, 'I never felt I was getting more than the sound of my voice over to him.'

Yet this detachment might have been expected, for throughout his life, from the very beginning, personal friendships had spelled only disappointment to him. His mother had died when he was born and his father remarried very soon afterwards.

Because George was then so neglected, he was removed from home by the authorities, and placed in a residential nursery. The young nurses who cared for him and the other babies were warm and affectionate, but they were very busy, with very little time to just sit, like real mothers, and enjoy a relationship with individual infants; and a child never saw the same nurse long enough to get used to her.

When he was about a year old, he was transferred to a foster home. This could have been his salvation, for here he might have found a warm and stable mother-figure, but unfortunately his behaviour was against him. 'Too difficult', said his foster parents, and he was moved to another couple. Time after time, this sequence was repeated, and at last the authorities gave up. He came back to a large barracks of an institution. Here there was stability of a kind – the stability of rules strictly enforced, of a timetable which went through its pre-ordained motions with inexorable regularity, day after day. It was a stability achieved by eliminating the capricious but rewarding human element almost completely.

One can only guess what might have passed through George's mind as he endured all this. To reach out to people time after time, only to see them slip out of reach again, must have been a very painful experience, for few things in life are as painful as unrequited love. It was small wonder, then, if George became disillusioned, and began to insulate himself against these disappointments by building up his life on an impersonal basis which excluded human relationships. Cut off, then, from communion with other people, it was only to be expected that he would be unable to feel with and for them, becoming a little callous, and that he should fail to absorb generally accepted ideas of guilt and morality, and generally accepted ideas about what is normal in behaviour and what consequences are likely to accrue to him or other people from particular kinds of behaviour.

George is now twenty-two, and already has a long record of irresponsible and often criminal behaviour, culminating at last in attempted murder. Punishment seems to be no use and psychological treatment not much more promising, for the psychiatrist has as much difficulty in getting through to him as do other people. Highly dangerous and apparently intractable criminals like him have been long recognized in both psychiatry and criminology under the name of the 'psychopathic personality'. Such a residual category is very tempting as a waste paper basket into which one can toss all the cases one does not understand, and with which one has been unsuccessful. And as it has always been assumed that the psychopath is incurable, one's guilt about one's failure is allayed.

But Bowlby with his concept of the affectionless character (affectionless in the sense of being unable to give affection, i.e. to make relationships with other people) has provided a way of defining the psychopath more closely, in terms of his behaviour and history. He has also given us more room for optimism than did earlier students of the problem, who saw the origin of the condition to lie in some innate defect rather than in infant-training. What Bowlby has taken on here is an enormous task: no less than an attempt to understand the sources of human sociality. As research continued, his earlier hypothesis about this proved to be oversimplified. Physical separation from the mother during the crucial stage between the ages of six months and two years does not (as Bowlby originally suggested) in itself lead to the development of the affectionless personality. Some children seem to have stronger innate instinctual needs than others, and therefore, when deprived of love, feel the lack more acutely. Much depends, also, upon what happens during the period of separation and in particular upon how much love the child receives from those who are in charge of him at this time.

Understandably incomplete though the theory of the affectionless personality may be, something very important and very relevant to an understanding of the psychopathic criminal is emerging here. If further evidence were needed, it can be found in observations made far from Western Europe – not among criminals and deviants but among normal, socially adjusted individuals, the Alorese people (studied by Dr Du Bois), who live on an island in the Dutch East Indies. When her infant is fourteen days old, the Alorese mother leaves him behind while she goes out to work in the fields. He is thus often hungry and almost completely lacks the tender relationship which the Western child has with his mother. If the child's crying becomes too incessant, he may be taken up briefly by some other woman who can no longer bear to listen to it. He may see his mother before work in the morning, and after work at night, but this can only serve to highlight his sense of loss during the day. The typical Alorese, deprived in this way from the beginning of his life, develops into an apathetic person, over-sensitive and mistrustful, and with real feelings of inferiority. He has no ability to make warm personal relationships, and nothing which would pass muster as a sense of right and wrong according to Western standards. The affectionless psychopath with his deprived early history is a deviant, often a criminal deviant, in the West, but in Alor his may be the normal and accepted form of personality development.

The impact of these new ideas upon our child-care methods during the past ten years has been enormous. It is now recognized as of the greatest importance that young children should not be separated from their mothers during the crucial first two years of life, and that if separation from the biological mother is necessary on social grounds, every effort should be made to find the child a mother-substitute to whom he can relate emotionally as if she were his real mother. No longer, also, are mothers discouraged from visiting their sick children in hospital. In the past, mothers were looked upon as unhygienic and inconvenient intrusions into the wards, upsetting their children, who would otherwise have settled down in the hospital environment. It has now been realized that what was called 'settling down', was often nothing more or less than a retreat into apathy, and that even if visits did mean much weeping on a child's part, at least this was evidence that the child's feelings were still alive. Following the recommendations to that effect of the Platt Committee, visits are now encouraged in many children's hospitals, though others find it difficult to break with the older, more austere tradition. Some go much further and urge mothers to come several times a day, to feed, bath, and play with their babies. In some of the more advanced hospitals accommodation is even made available for the mother in the hospital itself, so that she may live there herself until her baby is well again.

Such measures as these are important for the happiness of children who have been removed from their homes because they are either sick or neglected; but they play an important part, also, in the prevention of crime. For affectionless psychopaths, sometimes produced it seems by extreme maternal deprivation, though relatively few in number, are among the most dangerous criminals with whom our society has to cope.

Chapter 5

Unconscious Motives

It is from Freud that we have, in the main, gained our present sense of the importance of the early years of childhood, and of the basic conflict between the animal nature of the young infant and the demands made upon him by civilized society. It is not, therefore, surprising that the explanations of chronic psychopathic delinquency just examined in terms of under-socialization should have been developed by Freudians. The stress thus placed on man's biological nature is important; one has only to look at the opposition it has aroused in certain circles to realize how seriously it is treated even by its opponents.

We still have to examine those forms of criminality which result from the kind of social training we receive, as distinct from criminality arising from under-socialization. This brings into view what many would see as an even more important contribution by Freud to our understanding of human nature: the role of unconscious mental processes in our personalities, with the contribution which this implies from those same unconscious motives to the shaping of criminal behaviour. Where such motives are important, the reasons given even by criminals themselves for their behaviour may be wide of the mark – even if they honestly believe them to be true. They may be no more than rationalizations produced to render intelligible to the individual something in his behaviour which its unconscious origins would otherwise cause to be quite inexplicable.

Whether or not we do adopt such a technique of avoidance will depend upon the alternatives available. Because of the experience which the adult has had in the management of himself and of his environment, there are other possibilities open to him. If he wants something very badly which life just does not permit to him, he knows enough about the world to be able to find substitute satisfactions, which, while not giving him all he wants, do at least prevent him from feeling completely deprived. If something happens which makes him feel for the moment a little inadequate, this does not necessarily have for him the overwhelming implication that he is a failure, for he has had enough experience of himself to know that in other respects he can succeed. He may sometimes feel snubbed and neglected by other people, but this does not in itself mean that he will feel that he has been snubbed because he is unworthy of love – if, that is, he has experienced plenty of acceptance from people in the past.

For the infant, driven by strong and untamed biological desires and with no compensatory experience to speak of, life is much more trying. His instincts do not allow half measures; they call imperatively for immediate and complete gratification, and anything short of this is reason for panic and fury. To understand this, one has only to consider the feelings of a very young infant if for some reason he is not fed immediately he feels hunger. He does not yet realize that if only he can wait a little while, his hunger will be appeased. When this kind of thing has happened once or twice to him, he will come to recognize that he will always be fed, even though a meal may sometimes be held up for a while because his mother is not very well-organized, or because she believes in maintaining a rigid time-schedule for feeding and the clock has not reached the appointed hour. But until he has learned this lesson, all he knows is that he is hungry and that there is no food, and such a predicament to any animal spells starvation. This would be a desperate enough situation for anybody to have to face, calling for desperate measures. The infant, dependent and helpless as he is, can do nothing about it, and so the strong feelings which might otherwise find expression in some attempt to redeem the situation impose the most intolerable stress upon him. Feelings of such intensity just cannot be borne, and the child seeks relief by dispatching them to the unconscious, and becoming unaware of them. His anxieties about food are not going to be dispelled by such a stratagem. They will reveal themselves in a thousand-and-one ways, possibly in straightforward feeding difficulties, or in adult life in fear of unemployment or of not making ends meet.

But the process of feeding in infancy is also accompanied by sensual pleasure in the use of the lips and teeth and feelings of well-being which appear to give the child a sense of being loved and of being worthy of love. Pleasurable sensations are the first experience one has of maternal love, and easily come to symbolize it. Hence the resort of a child to the sucking of sweets or his thumb at times when he feels rejected. Harlow's experiments with 'cloth' and 'wire' substitute mothers have shown that the sensual experiences of mothering are of great emotional significance, even to rhesus monkeys, and that when upset or frightened, they will run to the 'cloth mother' for the comfort to be derived from touching it, even though all their food is obtained from bottles held in the metal framework of the other 'wire mother'. Even in later life, although we may not feel able to suck our thumbs when we are unhappy, we often seek other forms of self-indulgence instead. To the child whose lack of love has made him feel unsafe in a hostile world, possessions, as a means to or a symbol for sensual gratification, may be a powerful source of security, like the squirrel's nuts. It is not unusual for a disturbed child, or even a grown-up, to steal almost worthless objects, and then to hide them away in an attic, or under a carpet as if the thought that they were there was in itself a source of comfort to him.

Such a person was Dennis, a deprived child who had just left school and before taking a job on a farm was training for his future work in a hostel. The other boys in the hostel complained that their property was being stolen and eventually traced the thefts to Dennis. Without his knowledge they watched through the dining-room window as he opened up a hole behind the garage in the hostel garden, and took out an old raincoat. Inside was wrapped a motley collection of articles: money, a watch, a penknife, handkerchiefs, a diary — all the items of personal property which had disappeared over the previous fortnight. As he surveyed his hoard he looked happier than he ever was in his normal life about the hostel. Discussion with him confirmed how much reassurance he gained from having this secret treasure. To possess momentarily seems often to provide transient feelings of being loved to the deprived, but to have one's booty thus permanently available, to be handled and gloated over, seems to provide a kind of permanent reservoir of love, a kind of mother-substitute. But Dennis's mother-substitute in the hole behind the garage could never provide him with real love, and by thus assuaging his feelings of insecurity, enable him to grow out of dependence on her in the way that the normal child grows out of his dependence upon his mother.

An additional unconscious motive is often to be discerned. A child who steals may be not only stealing gratifications (such as sweets or money) by which he seeks to compensate himself for his lack of love, but may also be expressing his resentment at having been deprived in this way. The formula seems to be 'You haven't given me love as you should have done; therefore I am going to take it and so get my own back.'

One of the commonest results of the frustrations which training necessarily imposes is such anger. Both in the psychological laboratory and in the psychiatric clinic it is found that, although other ways of meeting frustration are possible, the commonest way in early childhood is likely to be with intense anger. As the frustrators are most likely to be a child's parents, and in particular his mother, who are essential to his physical survival and the main sources to which he must look for love, the direct expression of aggression towards them is bound to be inhibited. To be angry with one's mother is seen by the ego as dangerous, or even later on by the moral sense (the superego) as wicked, and the angry feelings are therefore repressed. Because they are unconscious and unexpressed, they continue unabated, and if frustrations are excessive, then the individual becomes an 'angry person', seeking a target for his anger outside the family. There are many such ways of expressing intense hostility, but one way is through violent crime.

This may consist of the wanton destruction of property, or of assault, or even murder. In some cases, where the anger is a result of the frustration suffered by the young child in his relationship with authority figures in his family (often, in European society, his father), the aggressiveness thus evoked in him may be deflected upon authority in general. Anti-authority attitudes of this kind may lead to nonconformity in religion, politics, or convention; but sometimes they lead an individual into a bitter and unremitting war against other paternal surrogates like the law and the police. Such a person can be a very dangerous and incorrigible type of criminal.

All of this, of course, is going on under the surface and people will often argue that such explanations are merely an attempt to find an excuse for a scoundrel, whose acts are much more easily explained as the result of avarice or vice. No one is likely to jump at such a suggestion more readily than the criminal himself. He will be glad to accept convincing rationalizations for his behaviour. The real explanation has already been found intolerable, and although the individual may have progressed a good deal in maturity since then, the earlier association would still be strong enough to deter him from digging it up again. Tied up with rationalization is the use of symbols to disguise our real objectives. Apparently innocuous acts or things have significance in our unconscious lives, 'standing for' some repressed wish, and facilitating a comfortable rationalization about it. Thus articles stolen, as in the earlier discussion, may be said to be symbols for gratification and, therefore, love, but can also plausibly be seen as objects which are wanted for their own sake.

We may therefore grow up in years without ever divesting ourselves of aspects of our infant personalities. This brings out still another feature of unconscious wishes. Most repression takes place in the early years, when, as has been seen, other ways of dealing with one's problems have not yet been learned. The wishes, being repressed, are unmodified by later experience, and therefore remain infantile, and so seem irrational and highly unlikely, to the mature, conscious mind.

But their irrationality springs also from other sources. The unconscious is concerned with primitive, instinctual wishes, and the ego, the conscious aspect of mind, with common sense and social adjustment. The ego develops mainly through the agency of the individual's early training by his parents, as a means to the ordering and taming of his instincts, so that he may fit comfortably into organized society. There is a fundamental antagonism between this rational function and the instincts of the unconscious which is bound to lead to rejection of unconscious mental contents as bizarre. And there is still another reason: because unconscious wishes and anxieties are distasteful and even threatening to the personal and social adjustment achieved by the conscious ego, it will seek to discredit them by any means open to it, of which emphasis upon their far-fetched and irrational character must be one of the most useful.

The infantility of many repressions has, of course, important consequences for treatment. If they can be brought into consciousness (the aim of psycho-analysis, and of many other forms of psychological treatment), they often lose their force, for the individual can recognize that he has long outgrown such wishes. At the same time, it must not be assumed that all repressions become irrelevant (if powerful) fantasies in this way when infancy is left behind. The homosexual who has repressed the fact of his inversion so that he is completely unaware of the motives which lie behind his preference for the company of members of his own sex is not relieved of his problem when he becomes aware of it. Nevertheless, he does at last know where his difficulty lies, and is able to take more of a share in shaping his own destiny. To be driven into behaving as we do by unconscious desires which we not only misunderstand but actually misrepresent to ourselves does not lead to a realistic approach to life. We are precluded by the unconscious nature of these motives from weighing them up (or the behaviour to which they lead) in a sober and sensible way. We are also so much the less masters of our own behaviour: more likely to blunder blindly or impulsively into a predicament which a better understanding of ourselves might have enabled us to avoid. The homosexual who is unaware of his abnormality often drifts into teaching or youth work, and thus unwittingly exposes himself to (for him) powerful and dangerous temptations. He may easily be drawn into overt homosexual activity, and if caught be treated then by the law as a criminal.

Although a person's early social training often seems to take the form of a struggle between the instincts, which drive him to seek gratification, and his ego, which makes him feel he must accept frustration, the process seems in essence to be one of maximizing satisfactions. To demand too much and too peremptorily in the real world is to risk rebuffs and the imposition of punishment. The ego may thus be seen as something more than a mere 'trimmer' adapting itself to whatever winds of opinion happen to be about, but as the instrument of a functional process through which human satisfactions are protected and extended. In time the reality-orientation of the ego is supplemented by the individual's emerging moral sense. No one would deny the importance for the explanation of crime of gaining some understanding of the origins and the nature of moral judgement.

Psycho-analytical research shows that this faculty (the so-called superego) arises from the child's absorption of the moral standards of his parents. In classical psycho-analytical doctrine, this development is said to be a result of the way in which the child, some time between the ages of three and five, resolves the jealousies emerging at this time within the family triangle of mother, father, and child – the celebrated Oedipus situation. It is not uncommon nowadays, however, to see the superego as developing less dramatically through a fairly lengthy emotional interchange between parents and child. It is the lack of such a prolonged relationship with the parents which probably accounts for the weakness of guilt feelings, i.e. of the superego, as of the other ego elements acquired through the agency of the parents, among the rough working class, and its almost complete absence in the affectionless criminal.

With the emergence of the superego, the ego becomes still less of an opportunist, for it acts now, not only on the basis of 'what will work', but also on the basis of 'what is right'. Many repressions will now be affected by the ego, but acting under the tutelage of the superego on the grounds of morality.

And, where any tendency for such repressed wishes to become conscious would previously have been accompanied by anxiety at the threat which the ego saw them as representing to its safety, the emotion now experienced would often be guilt instead.

If in the grossly deprived, the superego is weak, in others, as acquired in infancy, it is often itself a major obstacle to the personal development of the individual. It is, after all, not based upon the child's own individual evaluations, but upon the assumption of a set of values, taken at second-hand from someone else. Nor are these, often, very accurate, even as copies. We are all very apt to understand other people's emotions and motivations in the light of our own. We can have no direct experience of what is going on in their minds, and so, for example, must interpret a statement by someone else that he is 'happy' as meaning that he feels as we feel when we are happy. To project our own states of mind upon other people in this way is not necessarily misleading, but may be so if our own state of mind is very different from theirs. The state of mind of a young child is very different from that of his parents: he is very vulnerable emotionally, and only too easily projects his own strong feelings and wishes upon his parents. Thus he is apt to perceive parental prohibitions as much stronger than they are, and as a result to acquire a superego which is more censorious than ever his parents were. If his upbringing has been highly moralistic, the result, when this has been magnified into the infantile superego, may be to prohibit so many satisfactions as to gravely impoverish his personality and his life.

We all know people like this, living very narrowly circumscribed lives, to whom almost anything enjoyable is 'wicked'. This must not only reduce their own pleasure in living, and the contribution they can make to life, but also means that their inner lives are a constant battleground between instinctual wishes, and an ego acting under the lash of a puritanical moral judgement, to keep them in check. It is out of such acute inner conflict that neurosis arises, or alternatively unconsciously motivated criminality as another kind of neurotic symptom. The psychiatrist's objective in treatment must then become such a degree of self-knowledge on the part of the individual as will enable him to temper the severity of this despotic conscience of his. One of the signs of the mature person is that he has begun gradually to replace the irrational and second-hand moral judgements embodied in the infantile superego by a more realistic morality based upon ideas of right and wrong which he has evolved for himself out of his own experience. And this implies, also, that moral choices are brought out into the light instead of emerging, full-grown and unchallengeable, out of an unconscious mental process.

This view of human psychological development is built four-square on Freud's basic assumption of 'psychic determinism'. Personality, and even personal morality, are seen as the result of a process of development over which the individual has little or no control. The highly moral person is not so because of any particular virtue on his part, but because of the accidents of his early years; and instead of admiring him, we may often have reason to pity him as someone whose early training has taken away from him much of the capacity for the enjoyment of life.

The case of Fred Brown shows how irrational an unconsciously nurtured sense of guilt may be, leading even to criminality rather than to its opposite. He went into a tobacconist's to buy cigarettes, and when the old lady behind the counter recognized him and began to scream, he hesitated too long and was seized. Only a week before, it appeared, Fred had held her up in the street and robbed her of her purse. Now here he was, brazenly undisguised (or as she seemed to be saying, disguised as an honest man) in her shop.

Such behaviour on his part sounds very stupid, and yet Fred is anything but stupid. It was not a question at all of his being unable to understand; but he seems to be driven by something within himself which he cannot control. He has to go on committing crimes, and always seems somehow to place himself in such a position that he will afterwards be caught. Most of the last thirty years of his life have been spent in prison. He tries to explain it all away – mainly, it seems, to satisfy his own inner questionings about his way of life. So he talks about easy money, and not having to work, but he knows inside himself that his life is empty and aimless, and that he spends it either in poverty outside prison, or in privation and hard labour inside.

What has become known about his history throws a little light upon his problems. Fred as a child received little love from his parents. Then a baby brother arrived on the scene. All normal children are apt in these circumstances to be jealous of the new arrival, but because Fred felt so insecure already his resentment was extreme. His mother and father doted on the new arrival, and even called on little Fred to agree with them, saying, 'Isn't he a darling, Fred? Such a cute little thing, and so pretty'. Fred always smiled, but inside he was intensely jealous. His violent daydreams about the baby frightened him, and had to be obliterated. When they had been, he was able to be kind to his little rival, even though jealous feelings still persisted on the fringes of his mind.

Then a catastrophe occurred: the baby was accidentally smothered by the blankets covering his cot. To Fred, his death must have seemed like the enactment of his own unconscious wishes against his brother. He had never committed any act of overt hostility against the baby, but in the unconscious the desire to do so is enough. Fred has carried with him an unconscious burden of guilt ever since. Like the rest of us, he seeks assuagement of his guilt through punishment, but he commits crimes in order that he may be punished for an act which he has committed only in his own mind. This means that his guilty feelings are hardly likely to be relieved, no matter how much punishment he receives, for he is caught in a vicious circle, seeking punishment again and again, but never managing to cancel out more than his sense of responsibility for his current delinquencies. By comparison with the enormity of the crime which obsesses him, these, both delinquencies and punishments alike, are trivial. And the sense of guilt remains unconscious; all *he* knows is that he must go on offending against the law, and that somehow he always manages to get himself caught.

The conventional and common-sense way of dealing with misbehaviour is by means of deterrent punishment, but in a case like that of Fred where a criminal actually seeks punishment, it is no deterrent, but an invitation. In other kinds of case, also, the same is true. There is, for instance, the kind of criminal who commits offences as a way of denying unconscious feelings of inadequacy and inferiority engendered in him by early emotional neglect. Such feelings of inferiority have little in common with the more realistic sense of inadequacy which we all have when confronted by a difficult problem. For one thing, they are all-pervading: the individual feels, not merely unable to perform a particular task, but below-par as a person. Such feelings however are only vaguely, if at all, within his span of consciousness; he is aware only of a feeling of disquiet which makes him want to prove himself time after time. Criminals of this type commit offences in order to bolster up their own self-respect. Their crimes make them feel that they do count at last, and the longer their sentences (or the larger the headlines they achieve in the daily papers) the tougher and the more important they feel. But as in the case of the punishment-seeker, what they have hit upon is not a solution but a palliative. Their feelings of inferiority are unconscious, and continue unaffected by whatever they may achieve in the way of criminal notoriety.

Repressed sexual wishes are also a ubiquitous cause of criminal behaviour. Some reference has already been made to the problems of the latent homosexual. As obviously abnormal is the behaviour of the male fetishist who steals women's clothing or slashes their raincoats, as a way of satisfying sexual desires which, in their normal form, are not admissible for him.

Tendencies of this kind become more obviously a threat when they take the form of sadistic violence or arson. Such offenders having learned in infancy to see sex as threatening, because of its incestuous Oedipal association with their love for their mothers, repress this instinct in its natural form, and instead give vent to it in disguised symptomatic form. So a man who is otherwise impotent may achieve an orgasm, and consequent relief, in the course of a violent attack on a woman (not necessarily accompanied by sexual assault), or in watching the blaze from the shop or hayrick which he has just set on fire. In the notorious Leopold–Loeb case in the United States in 1924, two young men from well-to-do families who had found objects for their homosexual tendencies in each other, committed various crimes together before they jointly murdered a young boy. They had partly stripped the corpse and Dr Abrahamsen, who later had much to do with the paroling of Leopold after thirty-four years' imprisonment, suggested that the body might have been sexually violated after the murder had taken place. Abrahamsen points to some of the sexual symbolism in the crime. Acid had been poured over the face and sex organs. And the roles of the two boys in the crime corresponded to their roles in their homosexual relationship with each other: Loeb, the active partner, chose the weapon, and Leopold, the passive partner, the receptacle for the body. The poison-pen letter writer, often a maiden lady of unblemished reputation, in making obscene sexual accusations against her victim, is satisfying, in this curiously vicarious way, long-buried wishes on her part for sexual gratification. Thus at one and the same time she satisfies her forbidden sexual wishes and most convincingly denies that she has any.

Ever since Durkheim's famous study of suicide, it has been recognized that the most important single cause of this is a sense of extreme social isolation. In a recent very thorough and undogmatic piece of research into shoplifting, it has been shown that unconscious suicidal tendencies may arise from the same sources, but instead of leading to physical self-destruction, are expressed in a desperate act of 'moral suicide' in the form of stealing from shops. Shoplifters, though of many kinds, are commonly middle-aged ladies facing a crisis which threatens to leave them feeling neglected and alone.

One, who had been an orphan from the age of thirteen, had married early and without love. The marriage had not even provided her with companionship. The last of her five children had only just left home, and she felt life had no purpose for her. Suicidal tendencies had already expressed themselves in the temporary loss of her memory and in a road accident in which she suffered a minor head injury. It was at this point that she stole glassware and clothing from a large store. Others are

more like *mock* suicidal gestures, designed to bring a son, perhaps, or a spouse to heel – 'the hysterical motive of binding
some loved one to his allegiance'. One such had a son, towards
whom she was very possessive, but who was going to America.
She went shopping with him on the day he bought his ticket,
and then a few days later stole table linen and a tie from the
same shop. She was not short of money and did not want the
articles; and, significantly enough, her son's demeanour suggested to the researchers that it had all happened before.

Some psycho-analysts are now raising the question of
whether, especially in the case of crimes against the person like
sexual assault and violence, the victim may not be as responsible for the offence as the person who perpetrates it. The
crime, in other words, may be invited by the victim because it
satisfies some unconscious wish in him. There is plenty of
evidence of the existence of such symbiotic patterns. A familiar
case is that of the wife who is constantly beaten by the
husband, and who swears she will go away for good, but never
does. Her friends cannot understand why she stays, but in spite
of her frequent complaints, the ill-treatment she receives seems
to satisfy her unconscious wish to be dominated and hurt,
which itself dovetails fatally with her husband's need to have
somebody to dominate and to hurt. The study of alcoholics
shows that some are protected and even kept by their wives,
who suffer a good deal in other ways, also, from their spouse's
drunken behaviour. Yet they seem to need to have their husbands dependent upon them as much as their inadequate men-
folk need them to lean upon. At the conscious level, such a
woman may regret her marital lot, and indeed protest against
it very loudly, but her real feelings show in the numerous
obstacles she puts up against any treatment given to him, as
well as the remarkable lack of emotion she shows in the face of
one domestic fracas after another. Cases are not unknown in
which any abatement of the husband's alcoholism as a result of
treatment is followed by emotional disturbance or even breakdown on the part of the wife.

Is it likely then, that a person who is assaulted or raped
may have unconsciously wanted this to happen? Clinical

C.C.S.–4

evidence suggests that this is sometimes so: the criminal has been seduced, as it were, into committing his crime. Even a little girl, sexually precocious, may occasionally have invited in some subtle way the sexual interference which aroused so much hostility in the rest of us towards her violators. Where this happens, to treat the criminal as solely responsible is as unjust as our present policy of punishing the prostitute but allowing her client to escape scot-free.

One may also question, and in a more general way, the *utility* of punishment, where unconscious motives are behind criminal behaviour. In most cases they may turn out to be neurotic substitutes. A repressed drive may be allowed symbolical expression in the form of a neurotic symptom, so long as the patient suffers some inconvenience from his symptoms. The discomfort seems to be accepted by the individual's moral impulses as expiating the guilt he must assume for admitting the repression to consciousness even in this distorted form. Neurotic symptoms in the form of crimes may also be permissible only while expiation through punishment is insisted upon by society. In this way cases of 'criminality through an unconscious sense of guilt', like that of Fred, may stand as representative for a much larger group of 'psychological' crimes. Criminal justice is full of anomalies like these, and a critical appraisal of it, therefore, will be undertaken later.

Chapter 6

Criminals and Punishments

Any realistic approach to crime must accept that though the weight to be given to the personal or the environmental sides of the problem may differ in different kinds of case, both are necessary. Certain kinds of individual may react differently from the rest of us in the face of environmental stresses or temptations. Conversely, social environment being as important to all of us as it is, the same person is likely to behave very differently in different social settings. And as we have seen, the concepts of 'the personality' and 'the environment' are themselves anything but simple concepts or even permanently separate; for it seems that it is through an accumulation of environmental experiences, beginning with the very formative experiences within the childhood family, that personality itself is built up.

Much of this emerges if one considers (in the words of C. R. Shaw) the 'natural history of a delinquent career'. First of all, the individuality of an infant is apparent from birth; already he gives in the intensity of his response to stimuli, and in the amount of restless energy that he displays, some foretaste of the kind of person he will afterwards become. This is what the constitutionalists mean by temperament. By the correlations they have established between temperament and physique, they have made it clear that some part of temperament is inborn, but there is some doubt as to whether all even of those attributes present at birth are inherited. Eliot Slater has shown that even identical twins can display important differences in temperament from the very beginning. This cannot be due to heredity, and must therefore have arisen (as Slater himself suggested) out of the early environmental experience of the embryo in the womb. Bowlby's work on maternal deprivation also gives reason for assuming that some basic, structural responses of human beings may be shaped by early post-natal experience in the family.

This may be seen as the beginning of the child's psychological development, as contrasted with his constitutional make-up. The powerful pressures brought to bear upon him by his parents during these very formative years are bound to affect his sense of security and personal worthwhileness, as well as giving him an image of himself and of other people which must colour his subsequent behaviour. His personality, as distinct from his temperament, begins to emerge. Because of the subtlety of human relationships, we ought to hesitate to say that personal stresses are absent in any case of a problem child. A more intimate knowledge of the family life of the child usually reveals tensions of this kind.

But although it is possible to speak about the main lines of personality being filled in at this time, such a development must on the other hand also be seen as the unfolding of potentialities inherent in the individual's constitution. His intelligence, for instance, is bound to affect the sort of lessons he can learn from his familial experience. His response to that experience, and in particular the intensity of his response, will be governed by the kind of initial temperamental equipment with which he approaches it. To take a single example, frustration means more to the person with powerful instinctive needs; and his response to it, either in the form of anger or as a drive towards alternative satisfactions, must be stronger than would be the case with those whose innate needs were less imperative. Easy enough though it might be to attribute character-traits entirely to the particular family experiences which evoked them, this would therefore be misleading. At the same time, it is true that where such experiences were lacking, so would be the traits in question; the constitution plays its part, but its influence is not final or decisive. This is the kind of process out of which neuroticism arises, and also those forms of delinquency which seem to be merely symptoms of an underlying psychological malaise.

Whatever the relative share of constitution and of subsequent psychological stress in the process, the person is now beginning to emerge. It is as the kind of person he is becoming that he will tackle the problems of his life in society. The personally insecure person will tend to be 'easily led', because he must buy acceptance at all costs. The aggressively predisposed will tend to meet difficulties in an explosive and destructive way. The inhibited and self-controlled person will bottle up his feelings, subjecting himself to inner stress rather than taking the risk of discharging his discontent upon the world outside.

It is in this light that one ought to examine the effect of the social environment, the subject-matter of sociology, upon behaviour. It is in this way that the mass impellent and the individual selective element meet. The individual who feels rejected is more likely to seek acceptance from a group, like a delinquent gang or his neighbours, and to be more dependent upon it, than the person whose upbringing has been such as to make him feel more sure of himself. In general the total neighbourhood culture and the methods of child training will be in harmony, but social change, and especially rapid social change, can easily mean that expectations of gratification established by training, and actually realized in the traditional way of life, may be disappointed in the new social pattern. Already, personal stresses in some individuals may have reached breakdown level, but in the circumstances of widespread deprivation now being envisaged, such breakdowns could be precipitated in whole social groups.

In either case, one must continue for the moment to speak of breakdown rather than of delinquency. It has already been pointed out that criminality consists of socially defined forms of behaviour, and the conversion of breakdown into delinquency therefore calls for the further interposition of social influences. The problem child becomes a delinquent when his difficult behaviour takes the form of law-breaking. Whether it does this or not will depend in the first place upon the extent to which he is exposed to the possibility of breaking the law. It seems to be mainly because of their more limited exposure that women commit fewer offences than men; even nowadays, they spend much more of their lives within the protected environment of the home. Another of these group differences in criminality arises from the same source: because of a social code, among middle-class people, which prohibits the acting-out of one's problems, the middle-class person with problems is more likely to be a neurotic than a delinquent. The general climate of a delinquency-area provides a setting within which delinquency, at a certain level, may be 'normal' for all its inhabitants, but be productive of certain other kinds of criminality only in specially predisposed individuals.

The very fact of being involved in criminal behaviour, then, sets in motion certain kinds of social process. In some families and in some communities punishment and social ostracism may follow, and, according to the kind of individual, may either check or reinforce the delinquent pattern. The fact of committing offences may alternatively open up for the individual social opportunities and relationships which more and more imply the continuance of his delinquency. The first stage in this may be that he joins a delinquent gang, and eventually reaches an approved school. If, like Ben, he thus finds his way from a delinquency area into a truly criminal subculture, such as that of the professional criminal, then his continued criminality becomes a condition for the satisfaction, not only of the more pathological elements in his make-up but also for the meeting of normal human needs like a natural desire for social acceptance, for a reasonable livelihood, or for a stable and emotionally satisfying marriage.

How incorrigible a criminal may be thus depends in part upon how predisposed he is by the shaping of his personality in early life; but it may depend also upon how long he has been subjected to the later social pressures, emanating from the criminal life itself or from the artificial, criminal subcultures created by the authorities in their penal institutions. If the former is the more important, the services of the psychiatrist are called for: if the latter plays a significant role, nothing less than a wholesale reorganization of the individual's way of life will do, possibly as well, in some cases, as help with severe, personal insecurities or conflicts.

The end-product, the persistent adult offender, has received a good deal of research attention. Dr West found only twelve per cent of the habitual offenders whom he studied to be psychologically normal, and this minority seemed to consist mainly of well-adjusted professional criminals. This is in contrast to Dr Gibbens's study of Borstal lads, two thirds of whom he felt able to describe as mentally normal. One can see in this difference some reflection of the selective process which takes place, the less normal being more likely to continue in their criminality, while the more normal 'sow their wild oats' and then settle down. But some part of the high incidence of psychological upset among the older group must be laid at the door of their penal experience. Most of them had served long sentences of imprisonment, which experience suggests is rarely without its effect upon the personality.

But there is also plenty of evidence of prior personal and environmental maladjustment among them. In an inquiry by Hammond, for the Home Office, into the backgrounds of about 150 men whose previous criminal records had led to sentences of preventive detention, almost a third suffered from some physical disability. Only sixteen per cent had received any kind of vocational training during their lives. A surprisingly high proportion of habitual offenders, ranging from twenty-eight per cent to forty-one per cent according to the date of research, were found to have remained unmarried and of those who did marry, only a minority both preserved their marriages intact and went on living with their wives.

A life-long criminal is often seen as a dangerous and actively antisocial person, but Hammond's research among preventive detainees should enable us to bring this image into better focus. While many of them were dangerous men – house-breakers with a positive antisocial orientation – others were elderly petty thieves or frauds, equally unsuccessful as law-abiding citizens and as criminals. These are, of course, better described as inadequate, than as antisocial. Their behaviour in prison bears out this judgement: over three quarters of Hammond's preventive detainees had good or very good records while in prison. But this again is in part a result of the process of imprisonment itself. A man who has served many sentences soon learns 'how to do his bird'; a good record of behaviour in the institution is no indication of progress in rehabilitation. Here we have an early intimation of the damage which we may do by the very efforts we direct towards coping with criminality.

All this shows how little real progress we have made in our correctional work with criminals. But though it is being carried out in what is in many ways still little more than a penal system, our reformative aspirations have led, especially since the war, to the differentiation of a variety of ways of handling criminals. These various 'forms of treatment' must now be briefly described. Some of them, nowadays, come into operation even before an appearance in court. The police have long assumed the right to caution offenders rather than to charge them, and in recent years there has been a steady increase in the extent to which this has been done. Some local police forces go further, and through juvenile liaison schemes set out to do social work with some of the younger delinquents or pre-delinquents who come to their notice and whom they do not propose, at the moment, to prosecute.

Some forces are opposed, in principle, to the idea of cautioning and do not use the device; still more are doubtful about the propriety of allowing police officers, whose training is quite different from that of social workers, to do juvenile liaison work. The somewhat authoritarian ethos of the police is not at all consistent with the permissive and accepting attitude of the modern social case-worker, so that police social work ought perhaps to be of a different kind – having about it more of the flavour of the 'heavy father'. If this were accepted and officers were carefully chosen for the work and then given a proper technical training for it (as they are for other specialized functions like that of traffic control) it could be a very useful way of delaying a child's appearance in court. With the growth of child welfare legislation from 1933 onwards, there has been a tendency to assume that it is in the child's interests to get him into court and under the ministration of some public welfare body as soon as possible. Tannenbaum, however, suggests, with some show of reason, that a court appearance alters the image of himself which both the individual and other people have of him. He crosses a real frontier at this point, beginning to define himself and be defined by others as 'a delinquent'. Tannenbaum may very well be right in claiming that this greatly increases the difficulty of rehabilitating him.

An offender who is prosecuted and found guilty may be dealt with most expeditiously of all by means of a *fine*. Despite its defects this is bound to be the method of choice for the more trivial or technical offenders.

There is then a group of court dispositions which fall under the general heading of 'binding over'. The simplest of these is known as *absolute discharge*, and really means giving the offender a second chance. If the second chance is coupled with a proviso that the offender commits no further offences during a period of up to twelve months, then it is known as *conditional discharge*, and is in the nature of a suspended sentence. The original offence hangs over his head for the period during which the condition applies. *Probation* is also a suspended sentence but the shadow of the original offence may hover over the probationer for a longer period (up to three years), and punishment for it may materialize, if he breaks the terms of his probation order in some way, even if he does not commit another crime. The crucial difference between conditional discharge and probation, however, is that probation also involves the supervision of the probationer by a probation officer, whose duty it is on the one hand to keep the court informed of the offender's progress, and on the other hand to help him to make good – in the words of the law on this matter 'to advise, assist, and befriend' him.

Attendance centres are really a bridge between non-residential forms of treatment like probation, and institutional forms like prison or the approved schools. The offender is not taken away from his home, but is required to attend at the centre for a period, at fixed times in the evening or at week-ends. Hobbies, physical training, and citizenship are taught, and emphasis is placed upon discipline and good manners. Most attendance centres are for juveniles under the age of seventeen, and are run by the police. There is, however, one centre run by the prison service for the age group seventeen to twenty-one. There may be a case for the extension of this kind of treatment to adults, and one possibility along these lines is examined in Chapter 8.

The courts may finally decide to send the convicted criminal to an institution. *Detention centres*, like attendance centres, are at present provided only for juveniles. The young delinquent is sent to a detention centre for a comparatively short period of intensive training, which also, like that in the attendance centre, focuses on physical fitness and health, discipline and social deportment. The young offender sentenced to longer periods of institutional treatment will go, according to his age, either to an *approved school* or to *borstal*.

Finally, there is, of course, *prison*. Very largely because of the danger of contamination, it is considered to be undesirable nowadays to put young people into prison, especially in view of the various kinds of institutional treatment which now exist especially for them. The law therefore provides that if a court wishes to send somebody under the age of twenty-one to prison, it must state in writing that no satisfactory alternative is available.

Prisons themselves also vary a good deal. On the one hand there are the local prisons, locked and barred, and very mixed in population, and with the rather limited training programme which these circumstances and a lack of facilities and staff impose. At the other extreme are the training prisons, busy and constructive, and many of them open camps. The question of whether a man should serve his sentence in a local prison or in a training prison is supposed to be based upon his 'trainability', but it also inevitably makes a good deal of difference to the severity of the punishment which being in prison inflicts upon him. And this vital quasi-judicial decision is made not by the courts but by the prison authorities. Then there are central prisons for long-term prisoners, and these also vary from the open atmosphere of Ley Hill in Gloucestershire to the rather grim environment and regime of some of the old convict prisons.

These are the alternatives available, and, cautioning, juvenile liaison, and prison classification apart, the verdict will be in the hands of courts of law. In making their choice, should they be concerned primarily with what the criminal 'deserves', or rather try to see themselves as diagnosticians, aiming to prescribe that form of treatment which is likely to be most effective in turning him from crime? As a preliminary to a closer look at the penal system, it is therefore necessary first to examine the way in which the courts perform their task.

Chapter 7

Blind Justice

It will be apparent by now that although firm conclusions about the causes of crime are lacking, we do know enough to call seriously into question the customary moralistic attitude towards offenders. Some of them we have seen to be psychologically abnormal people. They are suffering from emotional disturbances, originating often in the very earliest years of childhood, which are illnesses in exactly the same sense as the more easily recognized physical diseases – and every bit as much outside their control.

We find it very much easier to accept this of the insane criminal than of the obviously sane person, whose behaviour seems normal enough, but merely wrong-headed, selfish, or malicious. Yet to judge him in this way is to project our own feelings on to him, to imagine that his emotions are as cool and easy to manage as ours, that he is as sure of his acceptance by other people as we are, and (like us) sees life in terms of opportunities and outlets rather than blocks and frustrations.

If we could see it all through his eyes, we might be inclined to take rather a different view. For we have much the same weaknesses as he, and can behave in much the same way. We sometimes lose our tempers, and though we may stop short of smashing other people's property, the violent or wounding phrase has the same psychological character, and often does very much more damage. If people are spiteful to us, we usually feel justified in 'squaring the account', if we can manage to do so. (Our attitude to the criminal has itself something of this character about it.) But while admitting and often trying to justify all this, we draw the line at admitting dishonesty, conveniently forgetting stolen time and notepaper in writing private letters during office time, the occasional call on the office telephone, the firewood taken home, or the occasional half-day away from work (for a very good reason of course) during the cup-tie season. And even the most moral among us see nothing wrong with making the best case we can for ourselves on our income tax returns.

Our proclivities are not, it seems, so very much different from his. Perhaps the difference is partly in the intensity of our response to these situations. Tied-up inside as he sometimes is, insecure and over-sensitive, he responds more explosively than we. Or sometimes, maybe, he is in another sense less master of himself than we are, more at the mercy of his own unconscious. If crimes are committed at the behest of his unconscious wishes, we are even less entitled to treat the criminal as a fully responsible person. And perhaps, committing the most opprobrious offences of all, the affectionless psychopath, psychologically mutilated in infancy, is prevented even from wishing that he could behave better, or accommodate himself better to the demands of society.

Yet not all of our criminals are psychologically abnormal. And an even smaller proportion, a tiny minority (though a very dangerous minority indeed) are psychopathic. Most offenders, in fact, seem to be distinguished from the rest of us only in having come from delinquency areas, and therefore in being willing to justify, and often to commit, a rather different repertoire of dishonest acts. If one has been raised in a city-centre slum in Leicester, one is twenty times as likely to be convicted of a criminal offence than if one had been brought up in a more law-abiding part of the city. Cliché though it may be, can one, when faced with facts like this, resist the temptation to say 'There, but for the accident of my birthplace, go I'?

These are, of course, subversive ideas. If we allow people to escape the blame for the bad things they do, we shall be entitled even to stop blaming ourselves when our behaviour falls short of what it ought to be. As A. L. Goodhart, Professor of Law at Oxford, has said, 'A community which is too ready to forgive the wrong-doer may end by condoning crime'. If people are not to be held responsible for their actions, how do we even set about the social training of our children?

The common-sense approach towards personal responsibility does seem indispensable on practical grounds. And as it has such an important bearing upon our attitude to criminals, it is bound to affect our feelings about what society should do with them when they are caught. Two main threads are to be discerned here. It is argued, first of all, that justice demands that they should be punished, and that the punishment should be proportionate to the crime. Secondly, it is argued that punishment is necessary in order to deter. When people talk about crime and criminals, these two attitudes tend to crop up time after time in the discussion, almost inextricably interwoven with each other.

The idea that a wrongful act should always be followed by some kind of punishment is deeply ingrained in our natures. It is symbolically represented by the Scales of Justice, and our judges devote much anxious thought to the problem of how much punishment a particular offence justifies in order that justice may be done as between the criminal and the community, and as between one offender and another. Even the culprit himself (unless he is psychopathic) is relieved of some of the burden of his guilt when he is punished. The idea of having 'paid for', or expiated one's guilt after punishment is strong in all of us. It has been observed that even murderers awaiting trial often sleep and eat badly and lose weight, but having been convicted and perhaps condemned to death, recover their tranquillity and with it their appetite and ability to sleep.

Such retributive views have always been favoured by organized religion. William Temple, when Archbishop of York, wrote: 'It is, I believe, the first moral duty of the community, and of the State on its behalf, to reassert the broken moral law against the offender who has broken it.' Lord Longford, speaking from the Catholic point of view, argues that if we can never call anything wicked, we cannot call anything good. He goes on to suggest that punishment has its value to the person who suffers it. 'Its medicinal, its restorative, its healing function, makes it an essential element in salvation.'

Most people would feel that justice is a very precious possession of the free society, not lightly to be tampered with. It is a fine ideal, but how is one to carry it into effect? How much punishment does a particular criminal in fact deserve? Should a thief receive a prison sentence which is proportionate to the amount of money he has stolen, or is stealing bad in principle, no matter how small the sum involved? And then what about the circumstances of the criminal? Are all equally blameable? This may not appear a very difficult problem: the courts could always take into account mitigating circumstances. But mitigating circumstances may not always be easily seen, and it may sometimes be very difficult indeed to know how much weight to give to them. If, for instance, unconscious motives play a major part in a particular case, it will be no easy task to prove it. And how much weight should be given to the fact that an offender was brought up in a delinquency area?

It must also always be remembered that it is not the sentence which constitutes the punishment, but the individual's feelings about it. A fine means very much less to a rich than to a poor man; a prison sentence much less to the introverted and isolated person, than to the gregarious soul whose life is only worth living if he is involved in a continuous whirl of social activity.

To carry justice into effect in our criminal law is obviously more easily said than done. What our judges in fact do is to ignore the subtleties, and instead enforce the *status quo* in their sentencing policy. They have (like all of us) their own peculiarities, and occasionally exhibit these in their statements from the bench; yet they are not entirely free agents. They are bound by precedent, and so must continually hark back to other cases. An appeal against sentence to higher court is also often possible. These safeguards undoubtedly reduce the idiosyncratic element in sentencing. They also, however, do more than this: they enforce upon a not unwilling bench a backward-looking attitude. Legal and judicial traditions are therefore hostile to new ideas, especially those derived from psychiatry. Judicial comments on psychiatric evidence are rarely friendly.

They are said also to represent dominant attitudes in the sense of the attitudes of the dominant class. This has always been the Marxist view of the institutions of the state, but it has also been put forward by non-Marxist writers. They see the law and its administration as a tool of the middle class for preserving their own norms of behaviour, and for punishing protagonists of any viewpoint which clashes with this. In particular, lower working-class standards such as those discussed in Chapter 2 are reprehended. Property must be protected at all costs. Physical assault is punished, but legal assault through litigation (out of the reach of the poorer sections of the population) is encouraged instead. On the other hand motoring offences are treated with tolerance, and often as a mere technical breach of the law. Yet, as Colonel Willett has shown, they are often, in essence, not so very different from other kinds of crime. Most of those convicted between 1957 and 1959 of causing death by dangerous driving or of driving while disqualified in the Home Counties police area, which Willett studied, had previous records of a clearly criminal kind, as had a not inconsiderable minority of those convicted of insurance offences, drunken driving, dangerous driving, or failing to stop after an accident. Canadian research workers cited by Colonel Willett found a much higher rate of social and personal maladjustment among drivers involved frequently in accidents than among accident-free drivers. Fining as a punishment is also obviously class-biased.

There is no suggestion that the law is, in this respect, more biased than the more informal practices of our society. The whole trend of our ruling culture is against the extreme neighbourliness and the attitude of living for the present which we have seen to be so characteristic of the rough working class in this country. But this only makes their plight in relation to the law the more difficult, for as 'wild, feckless, and interfering' they receive little sympathy from their fellow citizens. Mitigating circumstances, for instance, are not easily discerned when they are up for sentence. And they can adopt few of the more successful strategies for mollifying the Courts, like a previously unimpugnable respectability, the evidence of a fashionable psychiatrist, or an offer to send one's errant offspring away to school to 'make a man of him'.

The courts thus reflect traditional attitudes towards the criminal more strongly than newer ones, and tend to be class-biased into the bargain. They give also greater weight to hostile and punitive attitudes, than to more compassionate and constructive ones. Some might try to explain this in terms of the personalities of those who become judges, asking: what is it in a man that makes him willing to spend so much of his life as a professional punisher? We all, undoubtedly, when we have a choice, tend to gravitate towards particular occupations because we find the work congenial.

Lord Goddard, the former Lord Chief Justice, in an address to the magistrates of Somerset, after calling for the return of the stocks, went on to say: 'Short sentences are a misfortune, but many crimes only carry such short sentences. You must harden your heart at times. These people who plan the coshings, and the robbers of the pay-rolls: it is no good talking to them about reformation. They live by crime. The duty of the criminal law is to punish — reformation of the prisoner is not your business.' Not all judges have such extreme views as Lord Goddard, but, for instance, the present Lord Chief Justice, Lord Parker, is an admitted supporter of corporal punishment, and it is usually from the judicial bench that most objections are made to any proposals to ameliorate the lot of the criminal.

But in being punishers, our judges also faithfully reflect the attitude of the general public. Criminals are butts on to whom the rest of us can discharge our own angry feelings. We all have such feelings, engendered by the frustrations of infancy, and the irritations of adult life may add to them. To discharge them upon our friends and neighbours is not permissible, at least unless they give us due cause. The criminal, on the other hand, is a sitting target. He has given us plenty of excuse. We can hate him and punish him with a positive sense of virtue.

The position is even more complicated than this. We all have unconscious wishes to keep under control, and at times of stress or temptation this is by no means easy. The common solution then is to see these wishes as if they were in other people and not in ourselves. In punishing them, we therefore reassure ourselves about our own innocence, and at the same time coerce ourselves into good behaviour. The conscious ego must often be saying, at a level of experience below the threshold of consciousness, 'See what will happen to you if you do that'. We are able to give a concrete demonstration of the dangers lying in wait for ourselves, unless we are good, and maintain our repressions intact.

The idea of justice, as we practise it in our criminal courts, is, as we have seen, only a very rough and ready approximation to the real thing. Our devotion to the ideal is very laudable, but our inability to carry it into effect gives us no reason to be satisfied with it as the main aim of judicial policy. Indeed, perhaps we deceive ourselves in believing that we ever do seek justice wholeheartedly. Perhaps our real purpose is to punish, as a reassurance and as an outlet for our own emotional needs. If we have such needs, and they are as powerful as they seem to be, it is natural and understandable that we should behave in this way; but it seems highly reprehensible to us, and so we seek a more acceptable explanation and find this in the idea of justice.

All this must sound rather remote from reality to many. Speculation is all very well, but we have a serious crime problem, and have to do something about it. It may be that our ideas about justice are not only misplaced, but actually irrelevant. Instead, we ought to be asking what action should be taken in order that crime may be reduced. This is the justification for the deterrent punishment of criminals. Let us teach them a lesson, and at the same time make them an example to other people. The essence of the deterrent approach is that we should quite simply, *frighten* people into good behaviour. It is said to operate at two different levels. The convicted offender is to be deterred by his punishment from committing further crimes; and at the same time an example is made of him to deter the rest of us.

The idea of justice and the deterrent attitude both form part of the man-in-the-street's approach to the problem. He moves, without any sense of incongruity, from an approach based on justice to one based on deterrence, in spite of the fact that the two are quite inconsistent with each other. There is no reason to believe, if we adopt a utilitarian deterrent policy, that this will do anything to ensure justice as between one individual and another. If so, it could only be by accident.

But perhaps, as our more hard-headed pragmatists would argue, we can abandon the idea of justice as unachievable, and concentrate upon deterrence in the interests of the community. If they are suggesting here that we can leave values and ideals out of account altogether, some misgivings are in order. Quite apart from the fact that too severe punishments are likely to defeat their own ends, because people will not enforce them, we do not nowadays believe in capital punishment for trivial offences, or in torturing or mutilating the recalcitrant offender. It might pay (though early nineteenth century experience in this country throws some doubt upon that) but most of us would feel that the price was too high. Deterrent punishment may have its value, and as we have seen, it may be effective even at a very deep level in the individual unconscious, but it must operate within limits set by our belief in the right of human beings to humane treatment.

Within these limits, how effective is punishment as a deterrent? To pose the question in this way is to fail to recognize how very complex our crime situation is. Criminals, as we have seen, are of many different kinds. One type of thief, motivated by nothing more complicated than cupidity, may well be affected by the prospect of severe and fairly certain punishment. The incidence of crimes of this kind is likely to be reduced by a firm and efficient system of deterrence. Acts of an impulsive kind, like much assault and unpremeditated murder, are unlikely to be materially affected. Nor are cases in which the offence arises from deeply-rooted psychological problems in the offender – and much premeditated murder falls into this class. As extreme examples here, one might take the psychopath, and the criminal with an unconscious sense of guilt. The former seems unable to draw any conclusion for his behaviour from the consequences which it brings down upon him; while to the latter, punishment is not a deterrent at all.

The effectiveness of deterrent punishment undoubtedly depends upon the kind of criminal to be dealt with and upon how certain he is that if he commits an offence the punishment in question will follow. Unfortunately, there is, in most cases, no such certainty. Everything depends upon the likelihood of an offender's being caught and sentenced. It has already been shown that only about forty-four per cent of the offences known to the police ultimately end up in court, and even of these, a few secure an acquittal. But the number of offences prosecuted are no more than a fraction of the total committed, so that there seems to be, on the average, much more chance of an offender's 'getting away with it', than of his being caught. As the detection rate seems to be falling the certainty of punishment will probably not improve much in the immediate future. The average detection rate is not a very satisfactory guide here. Some offences have a very high and some a very low detection rate, and the former are bound, as a result, to be more amenable to a deterrent approach.

As illustrations of the defects of deterrent punishment, it is worthwhile considering very briefly the case for the reinstatement of corporal punishment for crimes of violence against the person; and the case for the re-institution of the death penalty for murder. Recent trends in violent crime have increased the demand for both of these expedients among certain sections of the public. Post-war evidence on the effectiveness of corporal punishment is lacking, but a government committee (the Cadogan Committee) immediately before the war reported that violent criminals who had received such punishment repeated their acts of violence more, not less, frequently than violent offenders punished in some other way.

Capital punishment can hardly be said to have a deterrent effect on those sentenced to it, but a main argument in its favour is its supposed effect in deterring many others who would, it is contended, otherwise be tempted to commit murder. The changes in the law relating to murder effected by the Homicide Act 1957, made an evaluation of it possible, an evaluation published in a pamphlet by the Home Office in 1961. The Homicide Act abolished the death penalty for all homicides except for a group, called 'capital murders': those committed in furtherance of theft, in escaping arrest, or escaping from custody, those which involved the murder of a policeman or a prison officer, or resulted from shooting or causing an explosion. There seem to be some obvious anomalies here. The burglar caught in the act, who hit a nightwatchman to escape, would probably, if the nightwatchman died, suffer capital punishment, while the calculating poisoner of a spouse or a rich relation would not. This has been countered by the argument that the Act would have a deterrent effect upon habitual criminals, making them less ready to carry weapons with them on a job. They would, it was suggested, be afraid of accidentally killing someone, and running the risk of conviction for capital murder. The Home Office report shows that on the contrary, such increase in murder as has taken place since 1957 is in exactly this group. The fear often expressed that, if the death penalty were relaxed for particular kinds of offender (as it was in the 1957 Act), murders by them would multiply, has been found to be groundless; it is among those for whom the deterrent, in all its horror, has been retained that murder has increased.

Deterrence it seems has its place, but it may be a smaller place than we have been inclined to think in the past. It will not solve our crime problem by itself, and it is morally suspect since it is concerned only with the protection of society, and not with the personal rehabilitation of the criminal himself. The modern concept of correctional treatment seems to provide a wider framework for attack upon the crime problem and one within which deterrence might find its proper role. It implies that we adopt such policies towards the criminal as are likely to change his behaviour, whether these are of a punitive kind, or whether they involve psychiatric treatment or social work.

The treatment approach is not free from flaw. It must operate within the same ethical limits as are applied to the narrower deterrent approach; not only must the punishments imposed be limited in their severity, but certain kinds of psychological technique of a 'brainwashing' variety are also not to be tolerated. Some recent work by experimental psychologists which suggests that criminals might be trained into good behaviour by a process of mechanical conditioning, in much the same way as Pavlov conditioned his dogs to salivate at the sound of a bell as if it were food, seems to fall short, in this way, of what is due to human beings in the way of decent treatment.

Whether the foundations of our moral and social order are likely to be threatened by the adoption of a treatment approach, as Professor Goodhart would have us believe, is open to more question. If the reformative motive remains strong in our treatment policy, then there is here a powerful moral impulse at work, implying that it is the purpose of a penal system to help people to improve themselves. The emphasis is upon the achievement of certain desirable forms of behaviour, with the positive assistance of society, and many will feel that this is an advance over the negative approach of retributive justice. The values of our society will surely be stressed more powerfully by giving expression to them in our penal system, than by merely punishing those who refuse to abide by them. The retributive attitude may even place us in an insoluble moral dilemma: seeking a moral end through acts which ethical thinkers from Socrates and Jesus Christ to Professor Hobhouse and Lord Russell have condemned as intrinsically evil.

But even a treatment approach may not be comprehensive enough unless we are prepared to extend its meaning. It is used, as a rule, to refer to the treatment of individual offenders, but some part of our crime problem, perhaps numerically the greater part, springs from forces at work in society at large. Our treatment efforts may have to be directed not only towards individual offenders, but towards communities, and maybe towards certain aspects of our society which give rise to conflict, or leave certain groups within it disinherited and resentful. We have, above all, to beware of any treatment approach, even of this broader kind, which sees the reduction in the amount of criminal behaviour as the only objective. To treat or deter minority groups within our societies so that they no longer break the law, without first being clear that the fault does not lie in the law itself, may merely be to perpetuate a form of cultural despotism, which rising crime rates had begun to threaten.

Chapter 8

The Courts on Trial

The traditional idea of criminal justice finds its most impressive embodiment in our courts of law. Even in the magistrates' courts, the shopkeeper from round the corner, the union organizer, the estate agent and 'little Johnny's teacher', lose some of their everyday familiarity as they take their places upon the bench, clothed in the power and dignity of law-givers. But it is in the pomp of the assize court that the vigour and power of the ideal of justice is really brought home to us. One gets (perhaps more in the course of the preliminary rituals than when the judge actually gives us a sample of his wisdom) a sense of a great and age-old engine of justice, powerful and all-seeing; of checks and counter-checks which it is impossible to evade, of an ideal of equity between man and man.

But could all this instead, perhaps be some kind of historical confidence trick? It has already been suggested that our idea of justice may be a rationalization of what is at bottom punitive behaviour. This would not be to argue that the idea of justice is a fake, but rather, that instead of taking it at face value, we might try to understand what needs it is intended to satisfy. It may appear then as a kind of collective psychological defence. As proof of the validity of our ideals, we are often inclined to refer to the sense of conviction that we and other people possess about them. Most of us certainly have strong convictions about the rightness of the ideal of justice. But all that a sense of conviction does is to prove its appropriateness for us: that in the present state of our emotional economy, such a belief has for us a very special and much needed part to play. But justice seen in this light is not merely the solvent of unrest within us; it is a positive outlet through which these tensions can be discharged in (as it seems to us) a constructive fashion. Through the idea of justice the bad things within us are transformed into something new and worthwhile. All this, so long as we do not look too closely at the outcome. For to stand the famous phrase upon its head and thus perhaps give it more validity : justice may more often 'manifestly appear to be done' than to be done in fact.

If, instead, the ethic of correctional treatment be accepted, our courts of law, which were so admirable for the administration of justice, are found to have much wrong with them as instruments of this new social purpose. For one essential part of this process, the identification of offenders (what we at present call the establishment of guilt), it is as effective as any machinery which is likely to be devised. At this early stage in the proceedings, the supremacy of law, the protection of the rights of the offender, the rules of evidence, and a judge who through traditions and training can stand above the struggle, are all important to ensure that the rights and liberties of non-offenders are preserved. But when it is clear that the prisoner in the dock *has* committed the offence with which he is charged, it is no longer a question of imposing a sentence which will ensure that justice is done, but of diagnosing the source of the trouble and prescribing treatment. For such a task legal training and devotion to the ideal of justice are not enough. An expert knowledge of the social and psychological sciences is necessary if anything approaching a correct decision is to be made.

It is no answer to say, as some of our judges like to do, that they have something better to rely on than the theoretical knowledge of the '—ologist' – the practical experience of dealing with hundreds of criminals in the course of their work on the bench. The plain fact is that they have little or no relevant experience. Useful experience consists of being able to try something out in order to see if it works. If we are to learn by experience at all, we must be able to 'see what happens'. Unless we do, we can never know whether we are right or not. This is precisely the position in which our judges are placed. They are continually making decisions on the offenders before them, but never have the opportunity of discovering whether their judgement was right or not. The high rate of recidivism among men who appear before our superior courts suggests that their judgement is more often wrong than right. Only the local magistrates, through their probation case-committee, have some chance (with that part of their clientele whom they place on probation) of making some rational evaluation of their sentencing practices.

The failure of our courts as diagnostic agencies can easily be seen in what happens in the case of insane offenders, where no one could reasonably dispute the relevance of a treatment orientation. Recognizing their inability to diagnose insanity, the courts say, in effect: We will redefine insanity so that even the psychiatrically naïve, such as we are, can be sure that those to whom it applies are in fact abnormal. This may mean that we shall leave out many genuine cases of insanity to which a straightforward lay and common-sense definition would not apply, but we shall at least be on the safe side in not allowing some malingerer to escape his due meed of justice. We may marvel at the idea that 'being on the safe side' in such a way as to run the risk of punishing an insane person who ought to be treated, should be seen by our courts as a way of ensuring that justice is done. We shall find it even more difficult to justify an attitude to treatment itself, which suggests that if the skills of the social diagnostician are beyond judicial comprehension so much the worse for them. Many of us would rather feel that, if our judicial procedure is so limited, so much the worse for it.

The definition referred to is that contained in the famous (or infamous) McNaghten Rules, formulated by British judges in 1843, but used in various forms in many countries of the world, as a legal criterion for insanity. Under the Rules it must be proved by the defence that 'at the time of the committing of the act the party accused was labouring under such a defect of reason, from disease of the mind, as not to know the nature or quality of the act he was doing, or if he did know it, that he did not know he was doing what was wrong'. (In Britain 'wrong' means forbidden by the law, but in Australia, for instance, it means morally wrong.) Thus, if a man stabs his wife with a garden fork, under the impression that he is cultivating his vegetables; or if, while realizing that he was stabbing her he believed that it was a legal prerogative of a husband to do this: the court would allow the plea of insanity, and commit him 'during Her Majesty's pleasure' to Broadmoor, where psychiatric treatment would be available to him. But if he knew what he was doing, and that it was a crime, the fact that he was too insane or psychopathic to prevent himself would not help him. He would be found guilty, and only escape sentence if the Home Secretary (a political figure, very responsive to waves of public feeling, usually punitive towards murderers) was willing to use his residuary powers to reprieve him. The irresistible impulse is the rock against which the McNaghten Rules founder.

This is of course a difficult problem for lay judges to deal with. To accept the 'irresistible impulse' as a defence is to throw the door wide open to all kinds of sane offenders, who might quite justifiably claim that they could not resist the impulses which came over them to steal, attack, or damage. The difficulty would be less, however, if we were not always so determined that sane offenders should be punished and not treated: in strict logic there is little difference between the two kinds of criminal. But even short of this, the problem would hardly exist if the decision on sanity were being made by a court which had some knowledge of psychiatric diagnosis, or had some competent and agreed advice on the subject.

The defects of our criminal procedure are not limited to the lack of training of our judges. It is possible to imagine their being provided with the technical information they need in order to come to a satisfactory decision. Something of the kind is often attempted by means of a probation officer's report, or evidence from a psychiatric or other expert witness. Even their efforts, however, are nullified by the combative procedure we adopt in our courts of law. One side makes a charge, and the other side contests it: no one is concerned to get to the root of the matter.

Thus in the criminal courts, both prosecution and defence are primarily concerned with whether evidence will help or harm their own case. Naturally enough, they try to present their cause in the best possible light, and choose their witnesses accordingly. Even expert witnesses are chosen in this way: a psychiatric witness would be selected because his views were such as to make the evidence he would give helpful to the side which is employing him. The questions he is asked by counsel, and therefore the scope of his evidence, will be limited in the same way. In fact, he ceases to be an expert witness, and becomes a kind of expert advocate, arguing the case of his client from his own special point of view.

This situation often does the greatest possible harm to the public image of psychiatrists. There is still much that is obscure about mental disorder, and differing points of view are quite legitimate. When, however, protagonists of these different points of view confront each other in court and give diametrically opposed evidence, the public (whose resistances to psychiatry are strong in any case) have every excuse for deciding that the whole field of mental science is bogus.

Psychiatrists are in a difficult position in court, also, because of the McNaghten Rules, which, as we have seen, are so narrowly drawn that many readily diagnosed forms of insanity fall outside them. The psychiatrist is thus in a position in which he has either to accept the McNaghten Rules as a satisfactory definition, which would hardly be in accordance with his professional duty when he knows that they are not; or he must continue to affirm that other kinds of case are also insane, and take the risk of being ridiculed by opposing counsel and eventually held to be wrong by the judge.

Under the Homicide Act, 1957, a plea of 'diminished responsibility' may be made by the defence in cases of murder. The defence has to prove that the accused person was 'suffering from such abnormality of mind (whether arising from a condition of arrested or retarded development of mind or any inherent causes or induced by disease or injury) as substantially impaired his mental responsibility for his acts and omissions in doing or being a party to the killing'; he is then sentenced for manslaughter instead. There has been no real increase in the number of cases dealt with by the courts as mentally abnormal since the passage of this Act, suggesting that there has merely been a transfer of cases from the plea of murder to that of diminished responsibility. The expectation that the new plea would open more doors to the recognition of mental illness in the courts seems to have been disappointed. The position may now, in fact, be worse than it was before, for the hazards of the McNaghten rules seem to have caused many cases which might have been dealt with under this rubric, and have led to a straightforward finding of insanity, to be presented by the defence, for safety's sake, as cases of diminished responsibility. They thus lead to what, for any case of insanity, must be the highly unsatisfactory outcome of a prison sentence for manslaughter.

But in cases like this, professional advice, though obscured and distorted by court procedure, is at least available. In less serious cases, and in cases where insanity is not an issue, the judge is likely to have to pass sentence with little or no guidance from experts. If what is under consideration is a sentence to borstal or corrective training, he must first consider a report from the Prison Commission – acting through the governor of the local prison where the offender has been kept while awaiting trial. Reports of this kind are compiled hurriedly, and with no proper study of the personality or the problems of the individual in question. In juvenile cases, the magistrates may have before them a report from the probation officer or from the Local Education or Children's Department. If such reports are to be available for the court hearing, they have to be prepared before the accused person has appeared in court and been found guilty. Many feel that, as he is entitled to be treated as innocent until found guilty, the authorities have no right to pry into his private affairs at this early stage.

The only alternative to these unsatisfactory expedients is to remand the offender while inquiries are made, as soon as he has been found guilty, but this is not always very practical. If the case is being dealt with at the assizes or quarter sessions, which meet rather infrequently, he might have to wait a long time, and even be remanded in prison for a spell until the report could be considered and sentence imposed. The question of whether he should be sent to prison or not may thus be settled in advance, whatever harm it may do to him. And there is reason to believe that a prison sentence does do a good deal of harm to certain kinds of offender.

More frequent sessions of the superior courts would help. Crown Courts, local 'branches' of the High Court with a permanent local judge and sitting very frequently, have been set up in Manchester and Liverpool in place of the infrequent assizes, but they may not have met with favour in official circles, as limiting the experience of judges too much to one area and to criminal cases. Wise judges, it is felt, are more likely to be produced by breadth of experience. And even if Crown Courts were a good thing, they would still suffer from the lack of proper diagnostic facilities. Cursory reports by the governor of the local prison, on the advice of his senior assistants, are just not good enough. Remand centres are at last being provided, so that men remanded for reports will at least be confined in a special prison, limited to individuals awaiting trial or sentence. As the history of children's remand homes has shown, this is no guarantee that skilled professional staff able to carry out diagnosis of the kind required would be appointed.

The judge, in any case, always has the final word. Some may feel that this is a good thing: that when the experts are finished, it is for the 'plain man' in the shape of the judge to apply his worldly experience and common sense to it all and decide what should be done. Unfortunately, common sense (where it is not merely prejudice in disguise) is no guide on matters that lie outside the common experience. Most of us would accept that we need more than common sense if we are to understand and to control the phenomena of outer space; we find it less easy to accept that the mysteries of what C. E. Hendry has called 'inner space' can be coped with only if we possess something as advanced in the way of technical knowledge.

Nor is team-work between a lay person like the judge and the expert really workable. The expert's view should be based on the best available information at the present time, and to return to the uninstructed judgement of a lay person like the judge for a final decision can only be to dilute and weaken a decision which ought to have taken into account already all the available considerations. This emerges very clearly if one considers the use which might be made in court of a new diagnostic device: *the prediction table*. Prediction tables are built up from the analysis of large numbers of cases which have been on probation, say, or in borstal or prison. It is possible in this way to determine what kinds of cases have, in the past, been most likely to succeed after they have been subjected to one kind of treatment or another. The table can then be applied to new cases, so as to decide which form of treatment gives the greatest prospect of success with them. There is no certainty, of course; only a degree of probability. Research suggests, however, that treatment decisions made in this way are much more likely to have a successful outcome than those based upon the unaided judgement of the court, or even on the highly skilled diagnosis of a psychiatrist or psychologist.

Because there is no certainty, and because the tables work out only 'in the long run', so that they tend to sacrifice individual cases for the sake of a high success rate over-all, social workers and others concerned about individuals have been hostile towards prediction tables. To meet these criticisms some of the protagonists of this method have suggested that they should not be applied automatically, but be part of the evidence on which the judge bases his own treatment decision. Immediately their validity is impaired. They are based upon the statistical analysis of past experience, and can be expected to work only if applied strictly. Other considerations which might be introduced, by the judge or even by the psychiatrist, form no part of the statistical analysis, and can only serve to interfere with the efficient application of the table. Insurance companies use similar methods in fixing their premium rates. On the basis of a statistical analysis of past experience, they decide which kinds of insurance call for high rates of premium to meet the high risk of loss. Their tables, also, work out only in the long run; they gain on the swings what they lose on the roundabouts. But having once established the criteria on which their premium policy is to be based, they are not prepared to allow extraneous considerations to be brought into consideration, no matter how relevant they may seem in a particular case. If they did, the statistical basis for their premiums would be disturbed, and only by chance could their total premium income then be sufficient to cover their outgoings.

In the United States, prediction instruments of this kind were developing before the war, as a means of improving the selection of prisoners for parole, or of offenders to be placed on probation. Professor and Mrs Glueck even made attempts before the war to forecast which of a group of prisoners were most likely to be lifelong recidivists; and since the war they have extended their work to young children, claiming to be able to predict the prospect of future criminality in over ninety per cent of them. In Britain a start has now been made with borstal boys, the tables in question proving to be more efficient predictors than borstal housemasters who knew the boys intimately for many months. A British prediction instrument for use in probation is in preparation.

If our penal system is to become an effective agency of treatment, better diagnosis is essential. This means that expert opinion has to be brought to bear upon sentencing policy in the courts, and it looks as though this is a function which cannot be shared. The implication of all this, though revolutionary, would seem to be clear. Some American states have accepted the logic of this position, and have taken the sentencing function away from the courts and placed it in the hands of a treatment authority of social science specialists. The judiciary are confined to the determination of guilt, and when this is done the offender is transferred to the treatment authority for sentence.

Even if confined to sentencing, such a treatment authority has many advantages. As developed in the United States, however, it is also responsible for the carrying out of treatment. It usually controls a diagnostic clinic, which provides the advice it needs for making its decisions, but it also controls most of the treatment agencies. It is thus in a unique position for correlating the forms of treatment provided with the needs of the current crime and correctional situation. Our magistrates and judges are often heard to say to an offender: 'If there were such a form of treatment, I would like to sentence you to it', or 'There is no room in a detention centre, so regretfully I must send you to prison', etc. The treatment authority is in a position to provide forms of treatment, as it finds them necessary.

It can also switch clients from one form of treatment to another, as their progress seems to call for it. A man may be transferred from prison to supervised freedom in the community, as he becomes better able to cope with a freer environment. On the other hand, a man who has already been allowed to test himself out at home, but seems to need supervision for a time, may be called in for a period of institutional treatment. Flexibility of this kind, which our system entirely lacks, may seem antithetical to the idea of justice, but is obviously desirable if we are to adopt a whole-hearted policy of correctional treatment.

Nowhere is the contrast between the point of view of justice and that of treatment more evident than in the use which must be made of the indeterminate sentence in a treatment-orientated penal system. We already have some traces of it in our own system. The borstal boy, for instance, is committed, not for a fixed time, but for a period of between six months and two years, at the discretion of the borstal authorities. To extend this kind of arbitrary control by officials may seem highly dangerous. Safeguards would undoubtedly be necessary. Nevertheless, to set a fixed period for treatment from the very beginning, without knowing how the patient is going to respond, is as foolish in correctional treatment as it would be accepted as being in medical treatment. We have only to develop the medical analogy a little further in order to see how ill-adapted our present methods are to a treatment objective. Instead of a doctor, we ask a man-in-the-street (for such our judges and magistrates, in this matter, are) to say what ought to be done, and having done this, we insist on carrying on with his decision to the bitter end, no matter what happens. Small wonder if our penological patients, at least, so often fail to recover. On the other hand there is reason to believe that an offender does need some kind of maximum to his sentence to give perspective to it. Without such a ceiling he tends to give up hope and fall into apathy; and he loses also the incentive to reduce his sentence from a measurable target lying before him. Some limitations on the indeterminacy of a sentence do therefore seem to be necessary.

Unlike the judge or the magistrate, members of the treatment authority can learn by experience. Their wrong decisions soon make themselves only too apparent in the success rates of the authority's treatment agencies. And because their failures do come home to roost in this way, they are strongly motivated to have as few failures as they can. Not so the judge. The probation officer, the prison governor, and the police constable have to pick up the bits after him.

Studies of our courts have shown the most tremendous variation in sentencing policy in different parts of the country. This is particularly marked in the magistrates' courts, where local and personal prejudices play a larger part than in the institutionalized and tradition-bound assize courts. So, it seems, if you are brought before our magistrates' courts for an offence (and the greater mass of our offences are dealt with by the local magistrates) what happens to you depends upon which particular area you happen to be charged in. This throws a rather curious light upon the claim of our courts that they are concerned with the administration of something called justice. Nor are local circumstances likely to vary enough to justify such differences, even in decisions based upon the idea of treatment. A properly organized treatment authority should be able to achieve a greater degree of uniformity than this.

To take away the sentencing power of our courts, and to hand them over to a non-judicial body, is a very revolutionary and, many will feel, a very dangerous step to take. Our courts may be inefficient in prescribing treatment, but they are organized in such a way as to safeguard the privileges of the individual citizen, and our judges are themselves trained and brought up in a tradition which insists that they see themselves not only as 'sentencers' but as guardians of our individual rights.

This difficulty seems real enough. Nevertheless it only arises because of our reluctance to see criminal behaviour as anything else but the action of a responsible human being. If we could see behaviour or difficulties like this in the same light as we regard mental or physical illnesses, we should see that our fears were baseless. We allow the expert, in the shape of the medical practitioner, to confine mental patients for a limited period entirely at his own discretion. An individual who has been found to be suffering from an infectious disease can be required to go into isolation for a time. In those parts of the United States where treatment authorities operate, the individual has first to be found guilty of an offence; the rights of the ordinary citizen are thus protected. But having been found 'subject to be dealt with', as it were, society assumes the right to subject him to any humane treatment which it has reason to believe, on expert advice, will be likely to cure him. On the assumption that his social maladjustment is a burden to him also, this is to his advantage as well as to that of society. Anything less effective would be unfair to both.

Most of the American treatment authorities deal either with children or with teenagers. For the former of these, we have juvenile courts. Juvenile courts in this country are better than adult courts, in that the magistrates officiating in them are chosen especially for their knowledge of or interest in children. Expert reports are also more often available to guide the court in its treatment policy. Attitudes also tend to be milder: punitive motives are often to be discerned in juvenile courts, but the treatment aim seems more acceptable in a court which is dealing entirely with young children. They nevertheless remain criminal courts, and are only slightly more effective for treatment purposes than their adult counterparts. Adolescents are treated more rigorously, being dealt with as adults, and Dr Mannheim, among others, has strongly urged that there should be a special court for dealing with them. Treatment authorities would be more acceptable in this country for dealing with children. Although a government committee (the Ingleby Committee) which recently considered this question has not recommended any real alteration in the constitution of juvenile courts, they could be converted fairly easily into treatment authorities. There would be no great public outcry about this.

Our insistence upon treating adolescents as fully responsible shows, however, how much resistance there would be to any proposal to remove older age groups from the authority of the ordinary criminal courts. Even in the United States, only California has gone so far as to set up an adult treatment authority. There is some logic in this. The child's character is still being formed, and even though we persist in holding adults as fully responsible for their behaviour, we could find justification on the ground of their immaturity for treating children rather differently. It is at least arguable that we should go further, and treat the problem of crime as a whole as one for treatment rather than blame.

The English are not renowned for their radicalism. We cling to our traditions, and never give up an institution if we can help it. Our courts, and the idea of justice on which they are based, are among the most powerful of the traditional beliefs which we hold. Over long centuries of political stability, we appear to have evolved a pattern of social life which provides a tolerable balance of restraint and expression for our collective emotions. We have, in other words, found a way of living together which is not too stressful. Not unnaturally, we want to preserve this comfortable state of affairs if we possibly can.

Some indication has already been given of the part which our criminal courts must play in this complex psycho-social equation. To take away from them their sentencing role would be to destroy their efficiency as agencies of social blame and punishment. We should then be left to deal with a side of ourselves that we had hoped was comfortably disposed of for ever. We should have to find other targets for our anger in place of the criminal; or failing that we should at last have to face up to the fact that we have a good deal of hate within us. Possibly even more threatening, we should no longer be able to project all our own antisocial strivings on to others. Blame being seen as a scientifically untenable and morally unworthy reaction, we should have not only to recognize our own darker side, but also to learn to live with it.

It would be unrealistic to expect this to happen. Human beings do not make changes of such magnitude unless they are sure that their vital needs will be at least as well satisfied in the new dispensation. It may be that the explanation of the greater willingness to change in America or Continental Europe is due to the fact that they still have to find a satisfactory *modus vivendi*; their changeableness may spring not from a greater willingness to give up gratifications, but from the fact that they have still to achieve them. Our criminal courts stand at the very centre of what might be called 'the scapegoat syndrome', but its value to us is going to make us equally reluctant to accept dramatic changes in any institutions which form part of it – our criminal law, our police force, our prisons, and even our correctional schools.

Nevertheless, some changes seem to be on the way. The recent Government Committee on the Business of the Criminal Courts (The Streatfeild Committee) speaks of courts as 'sentencers', meaning bodies concerned with the prescribing of correctional treatment. But in true British manner, the Committee proposes making them more efficient for this purpose without changing their structure at all. Attention is focused upon how the courts, in their role as 'sentencers', can be provided with advice and technical information, and here the Streatfeild Committee sees an expanding role for the probation officer. He is to become, more and more, the court's adviser on diagnosis and treatment. There are many possible growing points of this kind. For instance, the present advisory function of the prison authorities in connexion with cases under consideration for corrective training or borstal, will become much more useful than it is at present if the diagnostic services provided in the new remand centres are properly organized and staffed. Remand homes, serving juvenile courts, need to become much more effective as observation centres. And prediction tables are in their infancy; they could have the most revolutionary effect upon the efficiency with which our courts prescribe treatment.

Yet the final decision would probably remain with the judge and the magistrate. Whether the decision is wise or not will depend less upon the competence of his advisers than on his own ability to understand and to sympathize with the advice which has been given to him. We may have, in the end, to provide social science training for our sentencers, as the Germans do. And perhaps even more important, we shall somehow have to build up a closer relationship between them and the treatment agencies, in order that they can learn something from experience about the effects of the forms of treatment they are prescribing, and the kind of cases in which each is most likely to be useful.

Chapter 9

Criminals in Captivity

Most of us see prison as *the* punishment for crime. Of all the alternative forms of sentence open to our courts, it figures most prominently in the public imagination. Other forms of disposition, like a fine or a term of probation, are seen as acts of leniency : as relaxations of the full punishment of imprisonment, allowed because of some mitigating circumstances in the particular case. Fines may legitimately be seen in this way, for they are in essence mild deterrent punishments (though they are experienced as less mild by the poorer offender). Probation, however, is different altogether. It is a form of treatment, and in its impact upon the offender anything but a mere let-off.

Seen as alternative forms of treatment, prison and probation are most strikingly distinguished by the fact that the latter is treatment given while the offender is living within the normal adult community, while the former involves treatment in an artificial community set up for the purpose. In this respect, prison stands as representative for other forms of treatment which share the same institutional character. Although they may differ from prison in many ways, detention centres, borstal, and the approved schools are also residential communities, and present the same correctional difficulties and opportunities as does the prison.

It is as a community, then, that one must first look at the prison. It is a community in the sense that a group of prisoners live together within it for a period of time, and must, therefore, build up the kind of relationships between themselves which alone can make community life either workable or tolerable. Hobbes argued that without government, man's life was 'solitary, poore, nasty, brutish, and short'. Certainly without some accepted rules of conduct, a group of criminals living so close to each other would be bound to make life extremely difficult for each other. Inevitably, ideas about the kind of behaviour to be permitted do emerge. Rules of this kind are of course quite separate from the rules enforced by the authorities within the institution. The official regulations are devised for the control and management of the institution and its inmates; these rules spring, on the other hand, from the needs of the inmates who have created them. And as they are criminals, the rules are much more likely to reflect their own deviant values than those of the authorities.

In any community, social norms are sustained in part by the urgent need of members of the community to be accepted by their neighbours. The discovery that certain things are 'not done' means, for most of us, that from then on they are out of the question. For to do them would be to run a real risk of being cold-shouldered by other people, and this is just not to be borne. It is likely that the prospective offender who has a place in respectable society is more deterred by the prospect of being shown up before his neighbours than by the more formal punishments which might follow if he were caught in a criminal act. It has been found that church members are less likely to become criminals than other people, and this is often put forward as an argument for the moralizing power of religion. But as every church-goer knows, church membership is no proof of deep religious conviction; it is much more certainly a niche in society, membership of a community which is apt to be very hard indeed upon any member who gets into trouble with the police. Even the confirmed criminal cannot tolerate social isolation, and seeks his social satisfaction in the company of other criminals. The criminal underworld arises as much from such sources, as because of the more concrete advantages which a community can provide for its members, such as the provision of a trained labour supply and a market for one's products (or in this case one's loot).

In the prison community the risk of social ostracism is even greater, for here you cannot escape your neighbours. Your movements are so restricted that you have either to win the regard of the small group with whom you are allowed to make contact, or be shut out of society altogether. Only a very rash or psychopathically isolated individual would take the risk of non-conformity in circumstances like these.

What is often forgotten, however, is that prison staffs may, in effect, serve even longer sentences than their charges. A prison officer with forty years' service will have spent most of his waking life during that time within the walls of the prison or in an offshoot of it, in the shape of a group of staff houses. He is bound to be as influenced by the public opinion of *his* neighbours, as is the inmate. Staff attitudes in prison tend to be very rigid. It has often been remarked that the young officer, imbued by his training with an enthusiasm for new, reformative ideas, soon finds himself confronted by the most powerfully entrenched traditionalism among his colleagues in the prisons to which he goes, and within which he has to find a place for himself, not only as an efficient officer, but also as a neighbour and friend.

Observers of the prison scene, punishers and reformers alike, are inclined to concentrate far too much of their attention on the relationship between the staff and the prisoners. According to their point of view, either the staff are too soft or insufficiently vigilant on the one hand, or too punitive or insufficiently interested in reformation on the other. These attitudes may be less important in some ways than the relationship between prisoners themselves, or within the staff community itself. One cannot even begin to understand how the relationship between staff and inmates comes to be what it is, unless one first recognizes that the prison community is basically a divided one. Although there are many values held in common throughout the prison, and many points of contact between staff and inmates, the basic fact about the prison situation is that there are here two antagonistic groups, confronting each other from powerfully embattled positions.

The traditional interest of the prison staff member is in the maintenance of order and security. Society, for whatever punitive or psychological reasons of its own, has always expected this of its prisons, and they in their turn have therefore recruited men who find the enforcement of such standards easy and pleasant. Another way of putting this may be that the prisons have in the past recruited men whose psychological make-up is such that they are so disturbed by disorder that they must speedily put an end to it if they can. For some of us, disorder outside is too great a temptation to the dissident wishes within us to be tolerable for very long. Supported thus by pressures from the world outside and from our own psychological defences, the demand for the maintenance of at least the outward forms of order in our prisons becomes very powerful, and very resistant to attempts to change it.

But the demand is, on the whole, only for outward compliance. To ask for more would be to ask also for trouble. The staff can only enforce their will upon the inmates during the time the latter are under their direct surveillance, and the less the inmates' real needs receive satisfaction in their relationship with authority, the more of themselves they will put into their spontaneous community life, under the surface. A demand for order in our prisons is inspired by a morality and a punitive aim which is bound to be rejected by the prisoners themselves. The subterranean community life of the prisons is therefore a very powerful one. Springing from the standards of a criminal group, it is bound to be criminal in outlook. Seeing the staff of the institution as the instruments of a punitive society, it is bound to be anti-institutional, and anti-staff.

But open war would be unthinkable. For the inmates it would be impossible, and for the staff, at the very least highly inconvenient. The latter have traditionally been only too ready to 'let sleeping dogs lie'. It would, after all, be entirely in character for a person who is mainly concerned about not stirring up his own turbulent impulses to prefer not to notice what is going on underneath, so long as all is calm and quiet on the surface. The older prison officer has the utmost regard for the old lag, who knows the ropes and has enough sense to know when to conform. This places effective power in the hands of those prisoners who are most likely to be a corrupting influence on the rest. The young prisoner who begins by showing himself in his true light soon learns to dissemble; and the more he does so the more difficult it will be for the staff to reach him and try to rehabilitate him.

Recent studies of the prison community by sociologists have shown how this compromising temper on the part of the inmates expresses itself. Their ideal is the man who can show his hostility towards authority by his refusal to be deeply affected by it in any way. The trouble-maker is not welcome. He merely stirs up the staff to closer supervision, and increased severity. They value instead the man who can accept the limitations which compromise imposes, without becoming either coerced or seduced. He is, therefore, neither a rebel nor a suppliant, but a 'real man', firm in his loyalties, and secure in his beliefs. The 'real man' is the central myth of the prisoner community. The man who most nearly realizes this ideal in his own personality is the man who secures most respect from his fellow prisoners. But there are other recognizable social roles, which have to be played. One of these is that of the so-called 'merchant' : the man who handles the financial and trading relationships of the inmates. In English prisons his counterpart is the 'baron' whose currency is tobacco. Tobacco is greatly valued in prison and very scarce, and so serves very readily as money. With the aid of tobacco, the inmate can buy anything which can be obtained in prison. The baron carries on a lucrative business, maintaining the consumable supply of tobacco at his disposal by 'cornering' and smuggling, and then lending out tobacco at a high interest rate, and dealing unmercifully with any of his debtors who try to evade their obligations.

The honour in the inmate community may go to the 'real man'; the power (as, alas, is the case in the free community) goes to the man who controls the economic machinery. He is the man who can get things done, and who is able to manipulate the life of the community to his own advantage. It is an interesting commentary upon the differences in status systems and ideology between America and England, that in this country this dominant power-figure should be called a 'baron' and in the less feudal and more mechanically minded North America, 'a big wheel'.

This then is the complex community life of the prison. There are differences in emphasis in different kinds of prison. In the large closed institution, the picture drawn above is probably an accurate representation of what life is like. In smaller prisons and in open institutions, both of which facilitate personal relationships of an informal kind between inmates and staff, the division between the two may be less marked. In institutions for young people, like the borstals or approved schools, the characteristic features of the correctional community may be softened even further, dissolved by the multiplicity of personal contacts, by the genuine philanthropic impulses of the staff, and by the profound dependence of children (especially immature, deprived children) upon adults for protection and love. Nevertheless, the basic pattern is still to be discerned, laying its impress upon everything that happens in the institution.

Such a state of affairs is certainly not very favourable to the carrying through of a programme of correctional treatment. What may not be so obvious is that it is no more satisfactory, on the whole, as a basis for deterrent or even retributive punishment. The prisoners are not at the disposal of their captors, to be punished as justice or coercion require. They have their own highly cohesive and satisfying social life, which is out of the reach of their captors and of the vengeful or dissuasive hand of society. The powerful weapon of social rejection is lost. The prison provides a ready-made society and one within which the criminal can find a place only if he is unregenerate – a kind of officially tolerated criminal underworld.

This is the basic problem of the residential correctional community. In discussions on prisons and other correctional communities, much attention is devoted to the methods of treatment to be adopted. Topics like work programmes, education, religious observance, and social case-work figure large; and yet, in a sense, these are merely secondary and subordinate issues. In the end, the quality of the correctional work carried on will be determined by the nature of the community life in the institution. Whatever forms this treatment assumes, its true nature will be determined by the overriding factors of subcultural conflict and segregation.

Little is likely to be achieved unless the present highly integrated compromise can be broken down. How is this to be achieved? The most obvious answer is by the building up of more points of contact between the two sides. If a common arena can be found in which criminals can be themselves, and in which prison officers can hold their disciplinary impulses in abeyance, some real communication of problems and of influence may begin to take place. Something of this kind is now being attempted in the English prison system through group counselling, which is, in essence, merely a form of free discussion. The staff member in charge assumes a very permissive attitude, in order that the men may be encouraged to be open and frank; and, after a period of suspicion and testing-out, they seem prepared to be so. The sociological and personality problems which have given rise to their difficulties have then, at last, some chance of revealing themselves and becoming accessible to treatment.

The great advantage of the counselling group is that it enables criminals to be themselves within a prison without giving rise to extravagant outbreaks of violent or dishonest behaviour which the law-abiding community, with its own punitive residues to handle, would not endure for a moment. Instead all this antisocial behaviour is translated into verbal form. However trying it may be for the staff member in the group to put up with derision, insolence, and even outright hate, these can be accommodated within the framework of a secure and orderly institution, thus providing a spring-board from which further progress is possible.

That prison officials who are going to run such groups need special training almost goes without saying, but it may be that the training in question should be not so much in group counselling technique as in the ability to deal with their feelings when their own sore-spots are touched by remarks made by prisoners in the course of discussion. The officer to whom discipline is very important is likely to react badly to what he feels to be an insubordinate remark. The person with strong unconscious feelings of inferiority may find it very difficult to cope with the feelings aroused in him by hurtful or belittling comments made by men who, in the eyes of the public, are 'no more than common criminals, and deserve to be kept in their places'. Much experience of work with groups and in the control of one's own reactions in the face of provocation is required if one is not to bungle one's task as a group counsellor by reacting impulsively in response to one's own feelings rather than as a result of a calm appraisal of the situation in the group.

The prisoners will begin by assuming that the new method is merely a new weapon for use by the staff in the cold war between the two sides. A common reaction is: 'They're just trying to turn us all into stool pigeons; they'll get nothing out of me.' So the staff member must beware of bringing his normal prison community attitudes with him into the group, and thus confirming the suspicion in the prisoner's mind that it is the old pattern all over again, only rather more devious.

The responsibility is being placed here squarely on the shoulders of the staff. It is their responsibility, for it is they who are trying to bring about changes in their charges, and they must therefore cultivate their skills. But their own difficulties must not be underestimated. For this reason, the limited scope of an enterprise in which, say, only an hour a day is devoted to group counselling with each prisoner, has special advantages. Although the staff member has to assume an unfamiliar correctional role, and also to ignore prisoners from his own group and hold back his personal feelings, he has to do this for only a limited period of time. It is reasonable to expect that he will be able to assume a controlled, professional attitude towards his charges for so short a time without needing to change his personality and rethink his whole position. But more fundamental changes are likely to take place in him eventually. He cannot get to know the men under his care as intimately as the group makes it possible to do without coming to understand them better. As in all forms of psychological and social therapy, the therapist gains from the experience as well as the patient.

In being thus limited, group counselling stands in striking distinction to the other recent innovation in English prison methods, the Norwich system, which has developed as a response to criticisms of English local prisons. Based upon an experiment carried out in Norwich local prison, this aims at providing more opportunities for men to mix with each other outside their cells, and gives officers the responsibility of establishing a more informal advisory relationship with a small group of men.

It is certainly in local prisons that reforms are most desperately needed. They are first of all sorting centres for the prison system: a decision is made there as to whether individuals are likely to be suitable for transfer to a training prison – a regional institution (sometimes an open camp) served by a number of local prisons, in which the emphasis is upon rehabilitation. The others, the so-called 'untrainable', or those serving sentences which are considered too short to make training worthwhile, stay where they are, in the local prison for the whole of their sentences. Then there are the old lags. Central prisons, drawing their populations from the country as a whole, are used for these individuals serving very long sentences – of which the so-called 'life' sentence of fifteen years subject to remission will usually be the longest, now that preventive detention seems to be on the way out. Prisons of this latter kind include Dartmoor and Parkhurst, and contain of course many serious and incorrigible offenders. But the first year at least of such very long sentences is always served in the local prison, from which the offender is transferred, in due course, to the central institution which has been chosen for him. And until more remand centres are opened, the local prison has also to cope with a large floating population of men awaiting trial and sentence.

To try to do correctional work in a local prison with a heterogeneous population like this, many of them officially certified as poor prospects for reformation, is no joke. If one adds to this the fact that local prisons have been rather the Cinderella of the service, having what is left in the way of staff and training facilities after the training prisons have received what they need, it is easy to understand why they have settled for a mainly custodial role.

In our local prisons men spend many hours of the day locked up in their cells in idleness, instead of in constructive work or education. The work they are given to do is often monotonous and of little training value, like the manufacture or repair of mail-bags. Relationships with officers are extremely formal: concerned only with the giving and receiving of orders. Material conditions of life are sordid in the extreme. It is in the local prison that the inmate underworld is at its most powerful. To give inmates a more natural social life and prison officers a constructive social work function, as under the Norwich system, are very desirable aims. Nevertheless, to expect them to be successful in any except the smallest local prisons (and it is only in the small institutions that the Norwich system has so far been applied) is rather unrealistic. Established attitudes and a complex community life are not going to dissolve like magic before an attack mounted on such a narrow base. Too much of the old system is still left intact, and the parts which are changed do not affect the total structure of the prison community in any radical way at all.

The more experienced and institutionalized prisoner is not going to open up frankly in his relationship with the officer to whom he is assigned under the Norwich system; he will be as wary as ever. The prison officer himself, knowing that he is operating within a prison which remains, as a community, much as it has always been, and being subjected for long periods of time to the emotional strain which a counselling relationship brings with it, will find it difficult not to remain custodially (or even punitively) minded. The danger is that he will seek to make 'real' relationships with his charges, by descending in some respects to their level. Prison officers already share elements of a common culture with their prisoners: they often speak in the same prison slang, and display a common respect for the 'real man' type of prisoner who makes the custodial compromise a working proposition for both sides. It would be only too easy to be sucked in further, becoming identified with the inmate community, and so become useless as a factor making for change. It is likely that even more officers will be corrupted than in the past. The traditional detachment of the staff in the local prison at least protected them from this.

Group counselling does not attempt the same herculean task,

but experience shows that even it becomes less useful if it runs counter to strong trends within the inmate community. Men return from their group to the prison wing where they live to encounter sneers that the group is for 'nut cases', or even that group members are being used to spy on their fellow prisoners. It is therefore much better to try to develop a programme of this kind simultaneously with all the men who meet each other frequently in the course of their life in prison, say a particular wing or hall, rather than to spread it thinly over the prison as a whole.

If such a strategy is adopted there is every hope that the prison as a whole may eventually be covered. Then would be the time for a carefully planned attempt to change the prison as a whole into a correctional institution. Even then, the focus must be on the community rather than upon such individual factors as the relationship between a prison officer and a small group of prisoners. For the strength and the all-pervasive nature of the community pressures which made them such an obstacle to progress could make them a major power for good once group discussion had broken down old antagonisms and made old defences less necessary.

This breakdown in the traditional structure of the prison could be much hastened if its isolation from normal free society could be decreased. Prison systems the whole world over are highly introverted institutions. They carry on their lives behind high walls, have their own codes of behaviour and morality, and train many of their own staff. A prison doctor, for example, is a trained medical practitioner, but he is also a prison doctor sharing something of the culture and values of the prison with other kinds of prison official. A prison chaplain is no less sincere a Christian and no less hard-working a minister because he is employed in a prison, but one is conscious in talking to him about his work of some elements in his attitude to the men who form his congregation which unite him more with, say, the governor and his assistants than with clergy outside. The modern prison, especially the training prison, uses more and more specialists, for training, supervision of work, education, group work, social case work, etc. Many of them have been trained in the prison service. All of them have to find a place for themselves within the prison world. Like the chameleons we all are, they take on the colouration of their surroundings.

The adjustment is always to the prison system, never in the other direction, because the individual comes into the system alone and unsupported. It has become, as a result, inbred and conservative. It never has to face a real challenge from outside; when challengers arise they are absorbed, and eventually become 'adjusted'.

Why should a prison have its own medical service? Why should it not make use of the National Health Service, like the rest of us? Tutor-organizers, responsible for the prison educational programme, are supplied by local education authorities; it would help to break down the insularity of the prison if they were not allowed to specialize, but combined some outside teaching with their work with the prisoners. In two directions in particular much might be gained by bringing a breath of the outside world into the enclosed life of a penal institution. One of these has to do with the use made of the labour of prisoners. Especially in local prisons there is at present far too little work available to keep prisoners fully and creatively occupied. They work very short hours and, even for much of the time they spend in the workshops, are given such uninteresting tasks that they work reluctantly, slacking whenever they can. Labour is, in fact, being wasted. Meanwhile the state has to maintain them, and often, through National Assistance, their dependent relatives also.

For many years now it has been widely accepted that if possible men in prison should be able to earn wages for their work, which they could use to pay for their accommodation, maintain their families, save for discharge, and perhaps even pay some compensation to their victims. But desirable as this is in principle, it would be a bad thing under present circumstances in English prisons. So unproductive is prison labour, that the man could only be paid a wage as a kind of unearned dole. This would be good neither for his morale, nor for the national exchequer.

The first step must obviously be to make our prison industries more efficient. They consist in the main of small workshop units, using simple machinery, and organized on a nineteenth-century craft basis, rather than on the lines of a large modern factory. This is a result of the variety of vocational outlets which most prisons try to keep going at the same time, and it is often justified by the argument that prison industries are not intended to make a profit, but to provide training opportunities for the men. But for a man in prison, a most important part of his training is to learn what it is like to work in an efficient and properly run industrial organization : to learn to take orders at his work, and to have to work against the clock to meet delivery dates. To earn more or less money according to how hard he works. To be able to win promotion or suffer demotion, according to how well he does his job. Even to be sacked, and to find his income suddenly fall, if he cannot make the grade. And the production unit itself needs to be under the kind of spur which will make it enforce normal commercial standards of behaviour upon the men working in it : by having to meet, for example, competition from other business concerns.

What is in fact being proposed is that the small workshop system should be abandoned in favour of prison factories, each prison specializing in some industrial field or other and seeking a market for itself in the ordinary commercial world outside the prison instead of relying upon certain narrow and protected state outlets, like the provision of mailbags for the post office. Specialization of this kind need cause no restriction of vocational opportunities for the prisoners; within any industry there is a wide variety of possibilities, ranging from unskilled tasks to the most highly skilled.

Another objection which has often been put forward to such proposals is that it would be unfair for private industry to have to face competition from the prisons which they are paying taxes to maintain. When trade was bad it might even mean that law-abiding workers outside prison would be thrown out of work by this competition, with the result that criminals were in work while honest men were suffering unemployment. If one discounts the obvious retributive or deterrent element in all this, private industry would seem to have little to fear. Prisoners are not, on the whole, going to be very high-grade labour. And as a report in 1962 by a committee actually representative of industry, which the Government set up to advise it on this problem, pointed out, the prison labour force is so small in size that it can offer no threat of any importance to free industry.

A second area in which contact with the outside world would be specially valuable is in the field of correctional treatment proper. This must be in the hands of workers trained in both group and individual social work techniques. At present it is the practice to give special (and very limited) training in these methods to existing members of the staff of the prisons. Most of the training is given by the Prison Department itself. If instead, more practitioners were recruited from the professional social work field outside, and existing staff members who were to be promoted to new correctional grades were sent outside the prison system for their training, many of the attitudes and practices which now hamper real correctional work would be under strain.

This at least is not the kind of programme which can be adopted piecemeal. Nothing will do but the rashest audacity here. Our prisons will only be opened up if they are invaded, in this way, from all directions. Otherwise, the few lone explorers from the outside world who did penetrate into them would soon find themselves surrounded, sterilized, and eventually digested by the antibodies of the existing system.

Many of the defects of our closed prisons especially are due to their isolation from the life around them. A man commits an offence, and thus shows that he is socially ill-adjusted. When he is convicted, we put him into prison, and thus cut him off from the further experiences in society which alone would enable him to improve his ability to fit in. Even within the prison itself, we curb his social life in all sorts of ways; by locking him up in a cell, and by restricting his social intercourse with either fellow prisoners or the staff, and by subjecting him to a highly artificial framework for his daily work and his domestic life. Sexually he is required to become a monk; and a firm disciplinary system makes self-control entirely unnecessary for him. If he began by being socially maladjusted, he ends, after a few years, by being quite incapable of coping with normal life outside. We may then set out to provide him with special training just before he leaves, designed to make it more possible for him to live without the support of the institution. Having done so much damage, it is right that we should attempt to remedy some of it; but it would have been more sensible to have avoided doing the damage in the first place.

This involves treating a period of correctional treatment in prison as a specially designed form of experience intended to increase rather than to reduce the prisoner's ability to get on outside after he leaves. As many existing contacts with the outside world as are likely to be helpful would therefore have to be maintained. Existing restrictions on visits and letters, for example, would have to go, in their present form. The incursion of the outside world would be limited only to the extent that it was felt to be harmful to the prisoner's progress. Thus the prison might become a protected social situation, in which the task of adjustment had deliberately been simplified, in order that offenders, with their limited powers of adjustment, might be able to cope. Some limited isolation, carefully adjusted to the prisoner's own limitations, would then be justifiable. But as he became more competent, so more difficult tasks would be presented to him. More and more of the complicated problems of the outside world would be allowed to impinge upon him, until at last it was felt that he was ready for release.

In a prison run like this, after-care would be merely a continuation, outside the institution, of the treatment which had been begun within. From the very first day of a man's sentence, the efforts of the correctional staff would be directed towards increasing the area of his freedom, so that he might leave at the earliest possible moment. But it would not follow that when he was discharged, he no longer needed help. The task of the after-care agency would be to help him to continue to improve, to deal with the new problems which release, even from the most open institution, would bring him up against. For example, when released he would immediately encounter once more the criminal acquaintances who had previously been his friends and neighbours, or experience again the emotional stresses arising from intimate family relationships, to which he had previously reacted by committing his offence. To have visits from one's wife or parent while in an institution like a hospital or a prison, no matter how frequent or how natural the circumstances under which they take place, is not at all the same as going back to live with them once again. Ordinary family life, with all its daily irritations as well as its fears and insecurities, is a very different thing from the state visit.

If after-care is to fit thus into an integrated pattern of institutional treatment, it is difficult to see how it can be left, as at present proposed, in the hands of the probation service, whose connexions with the prisons are so tenuous. Continuity in treatment between prison and community (or borstal or approved school and community) calls for social work with the inmate, in or out of the institution, to be carried out by the same worker, or at any rate by the same service. Only so can the after-care agency expect to know all it needs to know about the offender and the adjustment he made while 'inside', and the institution staff all it needs to know about his history, social and family background, and release problems.

Responsibility for the whole process of treatment, and for its success and failure ought to rest securely on the same shoulders – and that must mean of the staff of the institution. It is only too easy at present for the prison department (for instance) and the probation service to blame each other for their failures; and indeed they may be almost justified in evading responsibility in this way, for they are hardly placed in a position in which they can effectively assume it. Nor is there now any justification either for continuing the present distinction between voluntary and compulsory after-care. All ex-prisoners should be subject to after-care, though whether this requirement was enforced, and how much after-care was provided in a particular case would depend upon the social work resources available and the need of the individual for continued treatment. The latter cannot be de-decided in advance, at the time of sentencing, but only as the case develops and the prisoner's problems and his response to treatment become apparent. More after-care help might be made possible in spite of limited resources, through the provision of day-reporting centres, analogous to out-patient clinics in hospitals, where suitable ex-prisoners might be seen as a group, and this would also provide (one would hope) a treatment-orientated peer group to counter the more antisocial group influences emanating from their social environments, and to provide them with acceptance and fellowship until they find a niche for themselves.

Such an institution might have an even wider utility if it could be expanded into a half-way house for some, nearer the beginning of their treatment, for whom, unsupported, the stresses of the free community would be too much as yet, but whose existing fragile adjustment would be damaged by incarceration. A full programme of correctional activities could be provided in such a centre, without either the expense or the disadvantages of residence. The 'out-patient clinic' would then begin to look more like a day hospital. The whole value of such developments as these is that they emphasize the necessity of slipping the offender gradually and imperceptibly back into society, if he is to have a fair chance of coping satisfactorily with the problems it presents to him.

But they will only be possible if after-care is made the responsibility of the prison service. And this more effective coordination of institutional treatment is going to call also for more localization in all our residential penal services. The present classification system, in which a prisoner or approved school boy may be sent many miles from his home to the institution which is considered to be most suited to his needs, must yield to a more sociological orientation in which the emphasis is placed upon proximity and increasing exposure to his own local environment and problems. There will be little lost in substituting the principle of controlled and constructive interaction between different inmates in place of an unrealistic attempt to provide a 'standard fitting' for a group of inmates classified as needing similar treatment. Human differences are not so easily disposed of.

Chapter 10

Criminals at Large

In the years since the war, confidence in residential methods of treating offenders, such as those examined in the last chapter, has been steadily waning. One result of this has been earlier licensing; wherever the penal authorities have had any choice, they have tended to shorten the period of time spent in the institution by releasing their wards, under the supervision of the appropriate after-care agency. Provision has been made for short-term treatment in certain approved schools and borstals. The minimum length of sentence which the Prison Department feels will justify training, rather than mere custodial supervision, has been reduced first from two years to eighteen months, and now stands at a year (under the Criminal Justice Act 1948, corrective training was assumed to require a sentence of between two and four years). Even preventive detention, intended to keep persistent and dangerous offenders out of the way for a long time, although a post-war innovation in its present form, has been used much less than it was at first, and sentences of preventive detention have been getting shorter. The general opinion is that it will soon be abolished altogether.

There are probably a number of reasons for this trend. For one thing, residential treatment is extremely expensive : not only has the prisoner, for example, to be fed and housed, but he is prevented by his incarceration from working to maintain his dependents, who thus often become a charge to National Assistance. And making sure prisoners do not escape is even more costly. The staff, especially in closed institutions, spend much of their time locking or unlocking cell doors, or keeping the men under observation; and a maximum security prison building costs more to construct than a palace (Everthorpe, completed in 1958, cost £900,000).

Penal institutions are bound to be a heavy financial burden, and at a time like the present, when committals to them are increasing rapidly, the burden becomes almost intolerable. At present we need new prisons, new borstals, new approved schools, and new detention centres. In June, 1964, about six thousand men in our prisons were still sleeping three in a cell, because of lack of enough separate accommodation. It is notorious among magistrates that places in approved schools or detention centres are difficult to come by; many a bench is forced to make some other decision about a boy because a place cannot be found for him in the appropriate institution.

The expense of new institutions might seem less burdensome if those we have at present were achieving good results. In such circumstances, it might even be good business; what, after all, is a few hundred pounds spent on training a boy in an approved school, if it saves the community the many years of drain on its resources which his adoption of a life of crime would cause? But the success-rates of all our penal institutions have been falling, until, now, not more than a minority of those discharged from any of them are likely to keep out of trouble afterwards. To take two examples for which figures are readily available, about sixty-three per cent of borstal boys and fifty-seven per cent of approved school boys are found guilty of further offences within a few years after discharge. It is even possible that the results would have been no worse if we had kept our money in our pockets, and had done nothing about these people at all.

As we have seen, penal institutions have very real disadvantages to surmount. Grouping large numbers of offenders together is a risky business. Unless we handle them very skilfully indeed, they are as likely to be corrupted as helped by the experience. But the deterioration in success rates over recent years must be due to other causes. Criminality is on the increase, and the greatest increase is in acts of a highly emotional and disturbed kind, such as violence and destruction. Could it be that the offenders entering our penal institutions nowadays are a more formidable proposition than those the institutions had to cope with in the past? Or to put it another way, are they of such a kind, more maladjusted and complicated, that our methods of institutional treatment have to change also, if they are to be as effective in the future as they have been in the past? This seems to be the view of many approved school headmasters and borstal governors, and is borne out also by borstal statistics based on the prediction tables, which show a steep decline in the prospects of success among new admissions. By 1963 only twenty-eight per cent were considered to have an even or better chance of making good on discharge.

But in addition to all of these reasons for the decline in reliance upon institutional commitment, there may be reasons of a criminologically scientific kind for believing this trend to be a very good thing. It is quite apparent by now, that criminal behaviour cannot be understood without some consideration of the background of the offender. Does he come from a delinquency area? As a child, was he a member of a delinquent gang? If so, it could be quite futile to try to reform him as a person apart from his background. He may behave well enough while he is away from home, but this does not prove that any change has taken place inside him, for conformity may be his defence against changing. Whether he has changed radically or not, he cannot return to his home and his old associations, with all the pressures they place upon him and all the stresses to which they subject him, without being in grave danger of reverting to the kind of behaviour for which he was originally committed. For then he is back where he belongs, amid familiar scenes and familiar faces. This society is not an alien one, a means for punishing him, like the institution he has just left. This is the way of life for which all his early training has prepared him. He would be a very odd person indeed if he did not take up all the threads of his old life once more with relief and pleasure.

If there is anything in the view that emotional disturbance has become more widespread among offenders, then the family as the probable source of these emotional insecurities looms larger than ever among the influences in the offender's home environment. The correctional institution leaves the family out of account. An offender may be trying to deal within himself, with strong hostile feelings against his father, or with sexual difficulties unconsciously centring on his relationship with his mother. He may feel deprived of love within his family, and seek to compensate himself through stealing. He may feel profoundly unloveworthy because of the lack of affection in his home, and set out to give the lie to the sense of inferiority this engenders in him by proving himself a tough guy through acts of thuggery. If any of these is the case, even the most enlightened institution cannot hope to deal with them satisfactorily.

Emotional difficulties centring on the family can only be dealt with realistically while the individual is continuing to experience the provocations and conflicts which arise for him within the family setting. To take him away from his family is to reduce their force, sometimes even to vanishing point; and as the level of emotional involvement between the offender and his family falls, so does the real problem of personal relationships in the family recede into the background. It is as if he left his problem behind when he went into the institution, put it into abeyance until he returned. The schoolmaster or the prison officer may then be able to do all kinds of things for him, teaching him perhaps good manners and the rules of physical hygiene, but he will be unable to cure him of his delinquency, for the cause of that has been left behind at home with the leather jacket and the tight trousers he wore when he committed his offences.

What our correctional institutions are trying to do, in so far as they are treatment rather than penal agencies, is to rehabilitate their charges in a vacuum. If their efforts meet with any great success, the result is likely to be some degree of institutionalization. The individual will have been detached from his natural social setting, and adjusted instead to the highly artificial society of the institution. This does not make him a more law-abiding person; it merely alienates him from outside society as such, and makes it necessary for him to seek institutional shelter again (and that usually means a penal institution) as soon as he can. But such an outcome is only likely if incarceration lasts for a long time. Most inmates make a superficial adjustment to the official norms of the institution, being more profoundly affected by their own peer-group, the subterranean, inmate community life. And often enough this inmate society embodies the deviant community standards in their home neighbourhoods in more intense and concentrated form, so that the offenders' social identifications and loyalties are strengthened rather than destroyed.

What may be affected strikingly, however, is their efficiency in sustaining any improved social role outside. They have to re-establish all their old personal relationships, which are broken for them by an introverted correctional institution. They have to learn all over again about work (or school) outside. They have even to re-learn simple skills such as how to behave with a girl, or how to balance a fragile china cup in a teashop, after the heavy mugs or metal tableware to which they have become accustomed during their sentence. These are the seeds from which the grosser forms of institutionalization will eventually spring if sentences are frequent enough or long enough, but even now they are sufficient to make him look with apprehension to the day of his release. Prisoners speak of 'gate fever' when referring to the increasing anxiety which they all feel in the last weeks of a sentence. In any case when the outside world looks as threatening as this, there is little chance of a man's renouncing that part of it with which he is most familiar and striking out for himself somewhere else. And when he does return to his old environment, he will feel very vulnerable, very anxious to toe the line and fit in.

The correctional problem is essentially one of helping the offender to adjust better to his own natural environment, to deal with both the stresses and the temptations which it presents to him. It may mean working with his family or with his gang as well as with himself. It may mean helping him to achieve some reconciliation between his membership of his own neighbourhood community (possibly in a delinquency area) and the demands made upon him by the wider society. It may even call for what the Americans call community organization, social work directed toward the neighbourhood itself, and aiming to help him to change by 'changing the street'. One British experiment along these lines was carried out in Bristol a few years ago by Dr J. C. Spencer. If such a major shift toward non-institutional treatment could be brought about, it would not be more, and might possibly be less expensive than present attempts to treat large numbers of delinquent individuals on a residential basis.

The correctional institution is not completely outmoded; there are certain kinds of case for which it is quite indispensable. Where, for example, the individual's background is too much for him – the conflicts induced in him by his family situation, or the pressures upon him from his delinquent acquaintances – the institution might have a protective function for him for a time, until he has himself been strengthened or his environmental difficulties have been ameliorated a little. Not dissimilar are the cases in which his behaviour has caused so much havoc in his family or among his neighbours that he has to be removed for a time in order to allow tempers to simmer down. Little success is likely to be achieved in adjusting him to his environment so long as people are so angry, and so justifiably angry with him. Sometimes placement in an institution may be called for because a particular offender requires treatment of a kind which cannot be given him while he is living at home. He may need a period of strict discipline inculcating in him good and regular habits. Such a programme is not in itself going to cure delinquents, but it is often a great help to the less intelligent offender whose other problems are exacerbated by his inability to run his life efficiently. Sometimes, again, a very rejected child, whose own home seems incapable of ever supplying him with the love he needs, may have to be provided with a substitute home within an institution. A foster home placement could be even better, but it is never easy to find people who are willing to accept into their homes, and try to understand, difficult children. There are many such special values to be found in a suitably organized residential institution, and which may call for a placement away from home in spite of the disadvantages which this inevitably brings with it.

There are, finally, two very practical uses which the institution has. Sometimes a criminal is so dangerous that he just cannot be left at large. The motive in sending him away, in such a case, is partly that of protecting society but this is not the whole story, for he may otherwise get into so much trouble and arouse so much resentment against himself as to greatly complicate the efforts of those who wish to help him. Then there is the question of what to do with the persistent offender when every form of treatment within a community has been tried and proved unsuccessful.

This last point reminds us that we are still very often in the dark when it comes to explaining why a particular person has become a criminal. Sometimes we think we know, and try out treatment based upon what we believe to be the cause of the trouble. This may work out successfully. If it does not there is nothing for it but a reassessment of the case, or even perhaps the experimental use of some other approach. Probation has failed with him; we must send him away from home and see if that does any good : this may sometimes be the kind of position in which we find ourselves. And the causes of crime are in any case numerous and very varied. On all these grounds, we need as wide a variety of forms of treatment as possible, including many different kinds of correctional institution.

The point to be made here, however, is that we must cease to look to our penal institutions as the main means through which the rehabilitation of our criminals is to be effected. They have their part to play in the penal system of the future, and a very important part it is, but the main emphasis needs to be placed upon domiciliary approaches. An institutional placement will only be made for special reasons. And even then it will be necessary for many of our institutions to make more contact with the real world outside, along the lines described in the previous chapter.

Probation is the most obvious nucleus from which a more extensive domiciliary treatment service could develop. Although the proportion of convicted delinquents placed on probation is smaller than before the war, nearly a quarter are dealt with in this way, amounting to almost 40,000 cases during

1961. The proportion placed on probation tends to decrease with age, presumably on the assumption that younger delinquents are more hopeful prospects for probation than those who are longer in the tooth (and possibly also in criminal experience). This may be true, but it would be hazardous to assume that the older offender, therefore, was more likely to respond to some form of institutional treatment than to probation.

The probation officer is engaged in the supervision of delinquents of all ages. He is a caseworker, who may try to get his probationer a job, or to clear up misunderstandings between him and his parents, get him into a youth club, or help him and his family to move to another house or a different neighbourhood. Or he may devote most of his efforts to the probationer himself, attempting to bring him to a better understanding of himself and his problem, and thus to modify his delinquent attitudes. These are the kinds of functions which need to be expanded and developed. But much development is necessary. Probation in its present form will hardly meet the bill.

At present, probation officers are all general practitioners. They are expected to do everything that is needed for rehabilitation outside the institution, and a lot of other things besides. They serve as social investigators for the courts, providing information, when called upon, to enable the judge or the magistrates to decide what sentence ought to be passed on the offender arraigned before them. They carry out inquiries into the means of persons whom the court have fined, or of men who have been ordered to pay separation allowances to their estranged wives or maintenance for their illegitimate children. They are thus able to prevent many men from being sent unjustifiably to prison for non-payment. They also do matrimonial conciliation: a wife who applies to the magistrates for a separation order may be asked first to see the probation officer in order that he might try to straighten things out between her and her husband. In some cases a husband or a wife, feeling that their marriage is going on the rocks, may seek his advice voluntarily.

Although some of these functions may seem only tangentially related to his main function of working with probationers, there is a real connexion between them. After all, many delinquents are so because of a conflict within their families, so that it must be valuable for a probation officer to gain experience of work with warring marital partners. It is probably also useful from the preventive point of view : a more oblique, but nonetheless real attack upon the delinquency problem, which in other ways he tackles through his casework with delinquents.

There is less of a case to be made for his continuing with the after-care work he does for prisons and borstals and for the approved schools. The former would be better organized as part of the total pattern of prison treatment; and although the probation officer may sometimes be well-placed for doing after-care with a boy discharged from an approved school who was formerly under his supervision while on probation, this earlier contact may not always be an asset if, for example, the boy feels that it was his probation officer's report which eventually caused him to be sent away from home.

In addition to all these extra duties, probation officers spend a good deal of time in court, making themselves available to give advice or information to the bench as it is desired. Then, when all this is done, they can turn to their probationers, and to the many different duties and responsibilities which probation casework brings with it.

Probation case-loads are not small : an average of about sixty male probationers are supervised by each male officer, and about forty females or little boys by each woman, representing a good deal of responsibility and a lot of work. On the optimistic assumption that the probation officer, after carrying out his other social work duties and doing all his office work, has fifteen hours a week to devote to interviews with delinquents, he would be able to see them, on the average, for not more than one hour a month each.

This is not very much contact, if the probation officer is to have the kind of influence which will change the individual's life to the extent that is required to turn him from a criminal into a law-abiding citizen. No probation officer would, of course, share out his time equally in this way. He tries to make some assessment of his cases: to decide which of them need the most attention, and which of them can be seen less often. As time goes on, and he feels the probationer is well on the way towards rehabilitation, he will tend to see him at less frequent intervals. But no matter how much skill he uses in thus husbanding his time, it is virtually impossible, under present circumstances, for the probation officer to do as much as most of them would like for the more serious cases in their charge. How could they be expected to take on the even wider functions for which an expansion of non-institutional treatment would call?

Two major ways have been proposed for relieving this situation. One of these involves drawing the ordinary citizen more actively into work with delinquents. Voluntary probation officers are already used in certain continental countries (notably the Netherlands), and have proved a great success. In these days of highly skilled professional social work, it would be an anachronism to hand over delinquents on probation to untrained volunteers without some safeguards, but if selected volunteers could be given some limited training, if the cases they took on were selected by fully-trained officers from their own case-loads, and if the work of the volunteers was then supervised by the professional worker responsible, many advantages might accrue.

Volunteers should be allowed to take one, or at the most two, cases of a kind in which a less professional but very frequent contact seemed likely to be most helpful. The man who needs someone to 'blow off steam' to, or the boy who needs an adult friend to give him support and encouragement: these are the kinds of people who are likely to get as much, if not more, from such a relatively informal relationship, as from the rather more intimidating relationship with the probation officer.

This latter relationship cannot help but be more intimidating. It is backed by all the power and majesty of the court which made the probation order. A probationer knows, also, that his officer has the duty of reporting upon his progress to the courts. That the courts continue in this way to follow the progress of a probationer is supposed to have some deterrent value. The probationer will 'watch his P's and Q's', for, if he does not, worse may befall him in the shape of an extension of his period of probation, or even replacement of the order by a more severe punishment. This watchdog function is often an embarrassment to the probation officer who takes his case-work function seriously, and finds that a probationer's wariness of him makes the establishment of a frank relationship between them a long-drawn-out business. The probation service has already been the pioneer in drawing lay persons from outside into active association in the work being done for delinquents. Probation areas have case-committees, consisting of lay magistrates, who follow the progress of the cases which they and their fellow magistrates have placed on probation. It may be the destiny of the probation service to carry this development still further in the future.

As the social sciences have, rather belatedly, begun to make progress, it has become inevitable that specialists in the handling of human relationships should have begun to take over many of the functions which were previously carried out, if at all, as acts of private benevolence. This has meant that social service has become more efficient. Because it no longer depends upon the whims of individual citizens, also, but is part of a national structure of social welfare, it has become more generally and more consistently available. Nevertheless something has been lost, in the way of warm-hearted informality, which tends to bring its own spontaneous response from those who are its recipients.

Perhaps even more important, something has also been lost for our society. When we seek to discharge our responsibilities to our fellow men by paying money, our taxes, our welfare-state contributions, or our donations to voluntary charities, instead of through personal service, both we and our society are the poorer. We have been robbed of our right to be of service and to give expression to our philanthropic impulses – perhaps at a deep level in the unconscious, to make reparation in this way for some of the bad things we feel we ourselves have done. Our society, in its turn, has moved just that much further in the direction of materialism. In a small way, the probation service may offer us an opportunity to call a halt to this tendency: offer us an opportunity to return to those ideals of personal service which both our Christian and our Hellenic heritages should lead us to cherish.

Yet probation remains traditionally an individualized approach to the offender, and as a result, a large part of the problem, that of his group affiliations, is hardly touched by it at all – except, that is, for the family. Social caseworkers do recognize the importance of the family in shaping the individual personality, and probation officers may sometimes spend as much time working with a wife or parents as with the probationer himself. But the delinquent's wider social environment is often ignored.

To consider young delinquents: a substantial proportion of them every year (usually well over half of the total), get into trouble as members of gangs. Even if several gang members are not being supervised by the same officer, he cannot help but recognize that the group has been a bad influence upon his client. However, he is usually very far from recognizing just how strong an influence it is. He often seems to operate on the assumption that he can, through his own relationship with the probationer, prevent him from running with the gang in the future. Of course a boy will promise to keep away from the others; he is not really in a position to refuse to do so. Neither, however, is he really in a position to keep his promise. The gang is not some alien intrusion into his life, but consists of his neighbours and friends, young people with whom he is growing up, and who represent the only sources of friendship and social recognition available to him. How can he help but go back to them again as soon as he leaves the probation office? And how much influence can the probation officer, seeing him so very infrequently and for such a short time, exercise on the other side?

The answer for a future in which many other kinds of case would be coming forward for non-institutional treatment, may be to teach groupwork to probation officers and also to add to probation social workers with other orientations. We must continue to have caseworkers, and indeed we must have also psycho-therapists who are trained to treat individuals even more intensively, but we must also have group-workers, who can work directly with gangs, and with other deviant groups within the community. We need also community workers who can operate on a very broad base indeed, helping neighbourhoods to find themselves as self-conscious social groupings, and eventually to want to take their place as members of our national life.

Community organization work of this kind has always formed an important part of American social provision; the British versions, the youth service and the community centre movement, seem naïve and irrelevant by comparison. Nevertheless these probably represent the best basis from which to make a start. The essential first step is a change in their orientation from the vaguely cultural and educational to the social. Their task would be to work with local groups, and especially with indigenous local leaders, so as to help into existence concern about neighbourhood problems and the will to do something about them. Such an essentially healthy shift in the metabolism of a community is bound to do more for it than merely to reduce its crime rate.

But a standing conference of all these social agencies, including the probation service (what, in some North American cities, is called a Social Planning Council) is also required if overlapping and conflict between them are to be avoided. To revert to the narrower problem of neighbourhood criminality, it will not be enough merely to supplement the probation service, as it exists at present, by other services providing group-work, neighbourhood organization, and so on. The assault on our crime problem needs to be highly coordinated. There must be a combined onslaught at all levels, where necessary. It must be easy for the emphasis to shift from individual to group or neighbourhood approaches (or vice versa) if a change in the situation, or a revaluation of it, seems to indicate this. Nothing will do but a properly organized domiciliary treatment programme, working on a broad base, and in a highly flexible but unified way.

By comparison with other forms of treatment, probation is highly successful, achieving about seventy per cent success. Nevertheless, it has to be remembered that our courts at present, place on probation those they believe to be the less serious cases. Also they usually see institutional treatment of one kind or another as the sequel to failure on probation. Prison, borstal, and the approved school have to try to do something for offenders with whom probation has already failed. Success rates on probation are therefore closely connected with the kinds of cases placed on probation. Benches in different parts of the country have different ideas about this, some being much more adventurous than others. Their success rates almost certainly vary as a result, showing the benches which use probation more freely as statistically less successful than their more timid brethren.

Any wider use of probation, in the kind of reorientated correctional system envisaged in this chapter, seems bound to cause probation success rates to fall. More difficult cases, many of whom would previously have been sent away from home, would be reported to the probation officer; and many of them, because their problems are mainly sociological, will be ill-suited to his highly individualized approach. This latter is really the crucial point. It is not merely their wider use of probation which may account for the more limited success achieved by some probation departments, but the extent to which the *kinds* of cases chosen are not those which are best suited to the methods used. The local areas in which probation is used least are therefore probably no better at selection – only more cautious. In fact very little is known about the criteria which should be taken into account, though it is to be hoped that current work on prediction tables for probation will help to make good some part of this deficiency.

Chapter 11

Youth in Revolt?

We are used to reading in our newspapers, of acts of vandalism or delinquency by groups of teenagers. Youths, strolling through a park late at night, suddenly, and apparently quite impulsively, decide to tear up hundreds of plants newly placed there by the municipal gardens department. A number of robberies occur one after the other; little is stolen, and the method of entry used is very amateurish. Eventually the police catch a small gang of boys red-handed, as they are breaking into a warehouse, and they readily admit the other offences too. Why had they done it? Not for gain, certainly; but as they put it themselves 'for a giggle'. Several boys queue up to have sexual intercourse with a local girl of a notoriously experimental disposition. Only when she baulks at going round a second time, and avoids compulsion by running to the police, does the incident come to light. Hordes of young people invade Clacton or Brighton on their scooters and motor-cycles, and terrify holidaymakers as they fight on the beach.

Because the press, and we ourselves, are likely to give undue emphasis to one or two striking incidents like these, they are not at all reliable as evidence of a general increase in teenage delinquency; but unfortunately the statistics bear them out. If we consider those found guilty of indictable offences among boys and girls between the ages of fourteen and twenty-one on a basis of numbers of offenders per 100,000 in the age group, this amounted to 2,090 in 1938. However, by 1960 this figure had increased to 5,136. In the last few years the rate has further increased to 6,529 in 1965 .

But it is not only in rate per 100,000 that teenage delinquency has been increasing. There has also been an increase in the proportion of our crimes committed by older adolescents as compared with other people.

TABLE I

Percentages in different age groups found guilty of indictable offences

	under 14	14 and under 17	17 and under 21	21 and under 30	30 and over	Total
1953	19·4	13·9	10·8	21·4	34·3	98·8
1965	11·5	17·3	20·8	24·0	26·7	100

Since 1953 there has been a shift in the age composition of the population, involving, for example, an increase in the proportion of young people age *17–21* in the population. But even after allowing for this source of error the share of this group in the crime problem increased by over one third, while that of the age group *30 and over* declined by one fifth, other age groups changing their shares only marginally. Crime is, it seems, increasing faster among our young people than among the older age groups. The adults' share of the total crime problem is gradually shrinking

The other major tendency has been for the amount of violent crime to increase more rapidly than such offences as simple stealing or false pretences. The statistics suggest that this new-found destructiveness is also mainly a teenage trend. Table II shows percentage variations between pre-war and 1965, in the share of each age group in different kinds of indictable offence (proportional increases in roman type, decreases in italics). These figures have been corrected for changes in the age composition of the population.

While the proportion of convictions for simple larceny obtained against young people aged seventeen to twenty-one has remained fairly constant, as compared with 1938, the proportion for violence against the person has risen dramatically. Breaking and entering, and damage to property, are other acts involving an element of violence in which the share of older adolescents has shown a sharp increase. Though the former

TABLE II

Percentages in different age groups of total found guilty of certain offences

	under 14	14 and under 17	17 and under 21	21 and under 30	30 and over
Serious damage	6	50·6	41·5	18·2	36·6
Personal violence	22	124·0	153·4	18·9	54·8
Sex	23·5	9·2	3·3	23·8	7·1
Robbery	28	107·6	8·5	12·2	12·7
Breaking and entering	14·6	3·5	64·1	76·9	1·0
Fraud and false pretences	144·4	3·3	77·5	34·1	24·0
Receiving	51·0	98·9	49·0	3·4	43·6
Larceny	12·4	80·2	9·5	21·3	11·8

has increased rather more among young adults and the latter among younger adolescents, the fact remains that both have climbed rapidly among the group *14 and under 17*. In conformity with this group's increased share in the total amount of crime (see Table I), its share of such non-violent acts as Fraud and False Pretences, and Receiving, has also gone up.

Similar conclusions were reached by F. H. McClintock's study of crimes of violence shows that the proportion of youths aged fourteen to seventeen committing these offences increased by 216 per cent and of those aged seventeen to twenty-one by 153 per cent, betwen 1950 and 1960. Our teens seem to be on the march. In our culture, adolescence has always been a time of stress and of resistance to the adult world. But covert resistance is now being succeeded, in some quarters, by what looks remarkably like the beginnings of open rebellion.

Most of these boys and girls commit their offences in company with each other. Well under half of the teenagers found guilty in the Leicester Juvenile Court in 1953 stood before the magistrates alone. Of 200 older teenage boys in borstal studied more recently by Gibbens, 143 committed their offences in company. And almost certainly some of these had accomplices whom the police had been unable to catch. Could anything more clearly indicate that this is an age group with a problem,

than these collective acts of defiance? But their group character is remarkable in another way. Adolescence is a time when
one expects the gregarious 'swarming' of the middle years of
childhood to be superseded by a growth in individuality. Yet
here we see a gang motive extending, among delinquents, into
the late teens. Years ago, Fritz Redl, a tremendously insightful
student of young people, argued that this was a regressive
tendency: a sign of emotional immaturity, a fear of growing
up and going forward in life, arising from emotional insecurity.
Many observers have noted how insecure and emotionally
deprived the members of delinquent gangs seem to be. T. R.
Fyvel spoke of the frequency with which they come from emotionally unsatisfactory homes; and Dr Peter Scott, a London
psychiatrist, after investigating the backgrounds of 151 boys
for the juvenile court, wrote that the real gangs he found
among them did not 'conform with the picture of healthy
devilment, adventurousness, pride of leadership, or loyal
lieutenancy, that is often painted. Gang-members who come
before the courts usually have a gross antisocial character
defect and come from homes in which the emotional atmosphere has been obviously disturbed and detrimental.' Could it
be that, deprived of love at home as they are, they cannot
strike out for themselves, but must go on clinging to each
other for acceptance?

Socially isolated individuals always have tended to gravitate
towards each other in this way. The criminal underworld, and
its echo in the inmate community of the prison, are examples
of this. Another is to be found in the Skid Row society to be
found in most large cities, through which social derelicts, like
alcoholics, drug addicts, and homeless unemployables, find
fellowship and at least the illusion of self-respect. Observations
of groups of infant monkeys by Harlow shows that even they,
if deprived of their mothers, tend to seek consolation in each
other; suggesting that this tendency may be part of the basic
biological nature of the higher mammals. In the most thorough
study ever carried out of the juvenile gangs of a great city, those
of Chicago, Thrasher showed how frequently young members of
immigrant families seemed to form gangs. Rejected equally by

the modern American society which they sought to enter, and by the traditional backward-looking European family which deplored their willingness to change, they had only each other in whom to find comfort.

It is not difficult to see why, if gangs are created thus out of deprivation, they should be hostile and destructive in their behaviour. Which of us would not be resentful, if robbed of something as important to us as love and acceptance? Dr Gibbens's research on borstal boys strongly supports the view that their gang-life is aggressive : he finds that aggressive behaviour was commoner among these gangs than any other form of delinquency. But young people seem to be trying to do something else besides strike back at those whom they feel have disinherited them. They seem to be saying no less emphatically : 'We'll prove that we are people who matter. We'll prove to ourselves that we are powerful. And we'll make other people take notice of us too.' This seems to be the meaning of the overbearing, boastful, power-drunk behaviour in which many adolescent delinquents indulge. As Gibbens says of his borstal boys : 'Fighting and the belief that they were being impressive was the main sustaining motive.'

Freud speaks of the earliest weeks of infancy as the narcissistic stage. As in the ancient Greek legend of Narcissus, who fell in love with his own handsome reflection in the water, the very young child is said to love only himself. His mother recognizes with joy the moment at which he begins to emerge from this self-containment of his, to smile at her and to begin to take an interest in her as a person, rather than merely as a source of nourishment and gratification. According to Freud, this egocentricity of the infant is a source of great security to him. Because all his own love and attention are lavished upon himself, he feels loved. In due course, however, he grows out of this early stage. His senses, and his ability to understand the world around him have matured; and as he begins to recognize that it is another person, his mother, who feeds, gratifies, and protects him, it would be natural, out of sheer self-preservation, that some of his self-regard should be transferred to her. He loves her, in the first place, because she is essential for his survival. But in loving her, he has voluntarily made a breach in his own defences. His mother's love for him must fill the gap, or he cannot but feel less loved, and therefore less love-worthy than before.

Generalizations about the state of mind of a child too young to talk must, of course, be highly speculative, but this is a speculation which does explain the feelings of unloveworthi-ness and inferiority which the deprived child usually displays. It also explains the frenetic preoccupation with proving one's potency and manhood among deprived delinquents to which reference has already been made. The underlying insecurity however, peeps out not only in arrogant violence, but in touchi-ness. To chuckle at their appearance as you passed a gang of Teddy Boys was to ask for serious trouble.

In an attempt to explain delinquent gangs, modern sociologists like Cohen, or Cloward and Ohlin, speak of a quest for status on the part of working-class youth, in a society dominated by the middle class. Prevented by the injustice of a class society from achieving this legitimate end, they turn angrily and violently upon their persecutors, or set out to achieve status within their own working-class society by means which involve a breach of the middle-class laws which they reject. This, as an alternative explanation, does account for many of the facts, such as the tendency for delinquent gangs to be commonest among the working class, and also provides a framework within which to understand the obsession of these delinquents with their own status. At the same time, many recent observers would agree with Zweig, who com-ments upon the declining importance of class consciousness in the English working class as their way of life comes to correspond more and more to that of their middle-class 'betters'. Reason has also been given in an earlier chapter for the view that class differences in delinquency are most likely to be due to differences in methods of child-rearing: the rela-tively deprived working-class child has little opportunity for acquiring the inner control, the tolerance of frustration, and the temperamental equanimity which a more prolonged re-lationship with his mother can give to a child brought up in a middle-class home. The feelings of unloveworthiness which such an upbringing may be expected to engender would then be more than enough to account for the status-hunger which these young people display; it is hunger based upon feelings of personal rather than social unworthiness.

J. M. Martin, an American student of juvenile vandalism, agrees with this conclusion. He writes that the families of vandals are 'characterized by more parent-child conflict and hostility than the families of other delinquents. . . . And finally vandalism itself, even more than other male delinquency, seems to be almost exclusively a group offence.'

One of the most remarkable features of the behaviour of these post-war gangs of young delinquents has been their interest in their personal appearance. It is not difficult to understand why they should want to wear a kind of uniform : the Teddy Boy uniform of a few years ago, the smarter 'Italian Style' of yesterday, or the sometimes (to adult eyes) grotesque Mod or Rocker garb of the present. Their solidarity is important to them, and a uniform both strengthens that solidarity and gives them continuous and reassuring proof of its existence. But their interest in their appearance goes much further than this. Boys, who seem otherwise to lay great emphasis upon their masculinity and toughness, will give as much thought to the cloth and cut of their suits as any woman. They will also spend hours and a good deal of money at the hairdresser's – and a good deal of time in front of the mirror – before going out to join their friends at the café, or out in the street. Not only does this show how skin-deep their male confidence really is, but it seems to hint at an enforced withdrawal on their part, back to infantile narcissism. Lacking love from other people, they must compensate by cherishing themselves. But unlike the affectionless psychopath so vividly dissected by Aichhorn and Bowlby, they have, most of them, though self-centred, taken too long a step towards seeking acceptance, to retreat entirely into isolation. They are caught instead in an emotional predicament, from which only their gang-membership and their delinquency give them relief.

But why adolescents only? Why, as Table I (p. 138) shows,

should children under the age of fourteen be so little affected? Leslie Wilkins speaks of a delinquent generation; the age-group who lived through the formative years of early childhood during the war, and whose social experiences at that time seem to have had some permanent effect upon their personalities and their behaviour. This view seemed rather more convincing a year or two ago than it does now. The group to which it referred are no longer adolescents, but young adults. Nor, on the whole, are they the most delinquent group any more; they have been replaced by a new delinquent generation, consisting of present-day teenagers, who are even more delinquent than they were.

It must be to the position of the adolescent in our society that we must look for enlightenment. His position certainly is difficult enough. He is sexually mature, and in societies less sophisticated than ours would be given properly sanctioned outlets for his sexual needs. We bring to bear all the moral, economic, and social weapons we can lay our hands on, in the attempt to delay the age at which he embarks upon mature sexual behaviour. His desire for adult autonomy meets with an even more confused response. On the one hand, boisterous or irresponsible behaviour meets with the rebuke 'childish', while on the other hand we resent any assumption of adult equality on his part. When, at moments of conflict over authority we ask him angrily, 'Who do you think you are?', we are asking him a question (even if it were not rhetorical) to which he could not know the answer. We have effectively prevented him from knowing who he is, whether child or grown-up. He is caught somewhere between the two, feeling very exposed, very vulnerable, very much in need of adult approval and support.

A survey by E. M. and M. Eppel indicates that many adults, even among those concerned with the welfare of young people, are very critical of them, seeing their sexual behaviour and their attitudes to authority as particularly alarming. For their part, all but twelve per cent of the young people in the study impose conditions on their acceptance of orders from other people – mainly adult authority figures at work. One girl, asked to describe when her behaviour merited praise, included revealingly in her list, 'When I manage to keep my temper when arguing with an adult.' There may be profound reasons having to do with our resentment at being overtaken and superseded, which accounts for our attitude to young people, but at any rate they are entitled to claim that they alone know where the shoe pinches. Exhortation is easy enough to those who are many years removed from the struggle.

We have come to expect disturbed behaviour from our adolescents, and yet anthropologists have pointed out that in other societies, like that of the Samoans, it is not an age of anxiety and conflict at all, but a period of smooth transition from childhood to adulthood. But then the Samoans do not place their young people in such an impossible dilemma; they have a recognized procedure through which young men and women can prepare themselves for adult life, and having proved themselves worthy, acquire at once not only the responsibilities, but the rights and prerogatives of the grown-up.

Meanwhile our teenager struggles like a fly to escape from the web in which we have him caught. To stay where he is, in this state of uncertainty, would be intolerable: he must move either forwards or backwards. On the whole, he has in the past found enough, if equivocal, adult support to enable him to move forward; but this seems no longer to be the case. One of the young people interviewed by the Eppels argues: 'I deserve praise when I do something that is worth a bit of praise. But people do not often praise teenagers nowadays'; and another says, 'Sometimes I go to a lot of trouble to do good. They do not even say "Thank you".' It is worth noting that fewer than one in three of them would go to their families for help when in trouble, and many of these comment on how much luckier they would be than many others in being able to do so. The Eppels conclude that 'this group of young people feels itself to be unjustly and sweepingly criticized by a hostile or indifferent adult generation that takes little trouble to understand their problems, and often misinterprets their behaviour to an extent that makes them feel hopeless and frustrated.'

Current teenage trends are probably one result of this situation. They imply that it is no longer only the rough working-class teenager who lacks adult approval but many others besides, and that it is out of this new situation that our new teenage problem is arising.

That it is a teenage problem, rather than merely a problem of teenage delinquents, is shown by the susceptibility to mass emotions that many young people seem to display. When outbreaks of violence occur among them, it is not enough to point to a leading nucleus of delinquent hooligans; for to be led is not to be compelled; one goes because one wishes to and because less inhibited individuals have been prepared to assume the responsibility of 'doing it first'. As Redl's analysis of emotional contagion in groups shows, a leader is responsible for our behaviour only in this last respect; his impulsive acts tip the scale for us, disturb an inner balance which is finely poised between impulse and self-control. So one gets a build-up in these scenes of riot and destruction. Small 'rock and roll' disturbances in cinemas grow into bigger ones; sometimes a town and a cinema which had already shown *Rock around the Clock* without any trouble was the scene of a wild disturbance at a second showing, because meanwhile there had been disturbances elsewhere. Ugly racial incidents such as those which occurred in Nottingham, Notting Hill, and in Dudley, began as minor clashes, but ended up by involving large crowds of young people. A battle between Mods and Rockers at one seaside resort is followed by a string of similar incidents elsewhere. The contagious spread of overt aggression through a large group of apparently pre-disposed youths is clearly to be seen in occurrences like these.

All this ought to give some indication of how we might set about trying to cope with the problem. To try to break up teenage gangs is a waste of time : their members need each other too much for that to be possible. We have, instead, to try to work with these groups, to guide and counsel them, help them to find more wholesome outlets as groups, and above all to give them acceptance and a little more of our time. It is only too easy to reject them out of hand; they are uncouth and sometimes seem almost viciously aggressive. They often frighten us just a little, and fear is never a good basis for relaxed and tolerant attitudes towards other people.

Therefore they need the coffee-bar type of youth club which the Albemarle report favoured, and in which the demands made on them are at first small. At least they are brought in off the street, under the benevolent eye of a well-intentioned adult. But they need more than this. They need the opportunity of getting their teeth into some kind of constructive task, through which they can assert both their solidarity with each other, and their need for significance. Merfyn Turner's experiment in youth work with a delinquent gang on a Thames sailing barge shows that so long as developments of this kind are not forced, but are allowed to develop gradually out of the young people's own felt needs and enthusiasms, they can be highly successful. If the old-style youth club failed in its appeal to young delin-quents because of the demands it made for self-discipline and self-improvement, the new-style club seems to err too much in the opposite direction. It certainly obeys the first principle of effective education in starting at the rather low level of the delinquents themselves; but seems to continue on the assump-tion that there is little or nothing to be done beyond this. Such clubs make a realistic attempt to capture their membership, but having done this seem hardly to know what to do with it.

Another approach which has proved its worth in the United States is that of assigning a youth worker to make contact with gangs in their normal habitat on the street. His aim is not to turn them into any kind of youth club, but to increase his influence with them up to the point at which they listen to what he has to say, and even occasionally take his advice. Many an act of vandalism and many a gang war has been averted by the skilful intervention of street workers like these. This is clearly the way in which our motor-cycle- and scooter-borne teenagers will have to be reached. The Mod and Rocker clubs already exist; society has to come to terms with that fact, and try to maximize their potentiality for good.

In whatever way efforts of this kind may be organized, they will be ineffective unless the youth workers involved are pre-pared to make genuine personal relationships with their young clients. Time spent in talking with them, not advising or exhort-ing, but just talking, being friendly, giving them the sense of being noticed and thought important enough to justify a little attention: this is the kind of thing which has some chance of alleviating a little the smarting sense of rejection and inferiority which is so strong in them. A youth leader may not stand in any blood relationship to the young people under his care, but their needs are great enough to make them look to him for parental affection and support if they believe there is any chance that he will provide these things for them.

This is, of course, only first-aid. We have also to try to understand why so many of our teenagers are deprived of parental support in this way. We may then come to the conclusion that we have a much bigger problem than teenage delinquency to tackle: a problem of changing social attitudes, and of a radical change in the role of the family in our society. More will be said about this in the next chapter.

But whatever the explanation, the problem is one which extends far beyond the boundaries of our own country. Gangs of destructive and angry young people are being reported from most countries of the world. From the *Tai-pau* of Formosa, to the *Bodgie* of Australia, from the *Tsotsie* of South Africa to the *Halbstarken* of Germany or the *Blousons Noirs* of France, from the *Stilyagi* of the Soviet Union to our own Teds, or Mods and Rockers, there is evidence of a new solidarity among young people, expressing itself in uniform modes of dress and in a smouldering hostility towards the adult world which occasionally erupts into wild outbreaks of violence. This problem seems to be most serious among those countries of the Western world which, since the war, have been able to raise the standard of life of the mass of their people to a high level. Could there be any sinister connexion between the 'affluent society' and our teenage problem? Is it at all possible that in becoming preoccupied with material progress, we have ceased to pay enough attention to the more personal, emotional needs which have to be satisfied if human beings are to feel adequate and fulfilled?

Chapter 12

Crime and Social Progress

In approaching the individual offender, whether for research or treatment, the intricacy of the total process of causation must be recognized. Looking, however, at crime as a social rather than an individual problem, as an arena for preventive action, the situation is a little different. Here the need is for a powerful social lever, through which a marked reduction in the level of criminality may be brought about. Because the emphasis has shifted from individual cases to mass phenomena, many serious cases may remain untouched. This may seem unfair and even thoroughly unjustifiable, but there is no gainsaying its practical usefulness.

Do such levers exist? In other words, do powerful causal factors exist in a sufficiently large number of cases to make it worthwhile for social policy to operate upon them, with a view to removing them and consequently reducing the amount of crime? What has been said earlier about the complexity of the causal process may suggest at first sight that we are only likely to discover these levers at a later stage, after diagnostic studies have been completed. But this is not necessarily the case. A particular factor like emotional deprivation may operate in many different ways according to the factors with which it is combined. In few of the cases in which it operates would it be sufficient by itself to explain criminal behaviour. Yet if it could be alleviated, so that it no longer represented a major factor in our society, then many cases of criminality which could only exist as such so long as deprivation was present side by side with the other elements, would be eliminated also. The factors remaining might seek some other forms of deviant behaviour, necessarily varied because they themselves would differ very much from case to case. This might pose a new problem for our society, but the problem of crime would, at any rate, become so much the less threatening.

Various possibilities along these lines have been suggested from time to time. The constitutionalists have proposed eugenic measures. Thus Sheldon, arguing for selective breeding, speaks approvingly of a possible change towards the treatment of 'reproduction as a kind of licensed and subsidized speciality instead of a *laissez-faire* competition'. The general tenor of the research on hereditary factors does not indicate that this is a sufficiently crucial or widespread factor to be of much use as a social lever. We may also, in the end, lose more by such a programme than we gain. Henderson has pointed out the similarity between certain kinds of life-long criminal and some highly creative persons, and implies that they are all basically (and sometimes congenitally) psychopathic.

But what would probably make a drastic eugenics programme unacceptable as part of any campaign of crime prevention is its incompatibility with many of the values which our society cherishes. Our conception of marriage and the family, of child-bearing and the relationship between children and their parents, are such that we tend to feel affronted by such a cold-bloodedly utilitarian attitude. Any preventive measure is likely to meet with favour only if it squares with the general drift of our culture.

Very different is the emphasis sometimes placed upon the improvement in social conditions. Crime, in all its various forms, is seen as greatly influenced by poverty, living in slums, and lack of social services. If social policy were directed towards remedying all this, the gain to our society would be considerable; but in addition, it is argued, crime would be bound to be lessened. We have little difficulty in accepting a policy of this kind : the amelioration of social conditions is accepted in almost every civilized country as a proper function for governments to assume. Though there is still more poverty about than some are willing to admit, the Welfare State has brought about a transformation of our national life, cured many social evils, and achieved a greater degree of social justice as between different classes in society than has ever been possible before. At the same time, it has had no noticeably beneficial effect upon our crime figures. Rather has its growth been accompanied by a parallel growth in criminal activities, almost as if it were itself a crime-producing agent.

While the Welfare State has seen to it that the economic cake is divided more equitably, post-war economic progress has ensured that the cake itself shall be a good deal larger. Although some groups (especially those with fixed incomes, like pensioners) have suffered, most of us are better off than ever before. But we are also more criminal than ever before.

It is possible that we may now have to reverse the usual hypothesis about the relationship between poverty and crime. We may now have to allow for the possibility that affluence can be a cause of crime. It is more difficult to believe in the latter proposition, than in the former. Theories like that cited by Vold that economic progress increases the opportunities for illegitimate as well as legitimate gains, are hardly convincing as an explanation of the current increase in teenage destruction. Nor even, as an explanation of the increase in property crime, does it account for the *relative* increase in this, as compared with legitimate activity; if such an accelerating tendency were inevitable, economic progress would be unavoidably self-destructive. It seems more likely that some pathological element is at work in the situation, an assumption which becomes more intelligible if one looks at the form which our new-found affluence is taking. To an extent that is new, in Europe at any rate, we seem almost obsessively preoccupied with its material aspects.

The phenomenon of the affluent society was explored by Professor J. K. Galbraith, but there are some features of it to which he paid rather less attention, notably the tendency for social status to be associated with material possessions. The up-to-date furnishings and the television set, and even the washing machine, the refrigerator, and the motor car are not merely becoming necessary to us for the sake of the comfort which they provide, but necessary in order that we may feel we can hold our heads erect in company. To lack these amenities is a sign of failure and a cause for shame.

The blame for much of this is laid, by some writers, at the door of modern, mass-production industry. Because industry, for its survival, requires an ever-expanding market for its products, it uses all the psychological resources of advertising and market research to persuade people to buy. In the process, social values of a grossly distorted kind are presented in a way which makes them very readily acceptable to us. Our manhood is persuasively shown to be affirmed or denied according to the brand of beer we drink. Our sexual prospects are settled by the hair-cream or the skin-tonic we use, and our social position by our car or our kitchen equipment. Our up-to-dateness is revealed to the whole world by the way in which we heat our houses, or by our willingness to give up 'old models' of almost anything in exchange for the latest version – which may differ from its predecessor in hardly any important functional respect. The inescapable logic of mass production sets in motion a powerful process of indoctrination, in which material acquisition is extolled as the most important thing in life : the solvent of our deepest anxieties, and the means through which all our yearnings may be satisfied.

Mass production has certainly to be taken into account, but it may itself be only part of a wider problem : that of the mass society, also organized for efficiency on the basis of standardized uniformity, in which human beings as cogs in the social machine must operate with the unfailing uniformity of cogs. Large-scale industry expects them, as workers, to fit into the overall pattern laid down by the needs of the productive process, every bit as much as it expects them to fit in as consumers. 'Workers' become a 'labour force', and their relationship to their work begins to be expressed largely in monetary terms. The great city, because of its size, can provide a dazzling array of amenities; but at the cost of losing sight of the individual in an anonymous army of commuters. As will be seen, even the Welfare State suffers from the same disease. And money is the great common denominator to which everything can be reduced : the agency through which universal standardization can be achieved. It can become both the end and the means.

However it has come about, the material is replacing the human as the overriding social value and, because (as we have seen) the former is no real compensation for the latter, the hunger for possessions becomes insatiable : material acquisition becomes all-important. As the government survey of 'Social Changes in Britain', made public towards the end of 1962, puts it, we suffer from a 'malaise which is perhaps too simply diagnosed as a desire, among the newly-affluent for more money quickly. It is more probably a basic discontent with what has become very strongly an era of materialism, and this discontent expresses itself in a grasping after immense wealth.'

This trend is well-documented by the survey : 'Three out of every four households now have a vacuum cleaner, two out of every five a washing machine, and one in three a refrigerator', most of it on hire purchase. Money is thus bound to loom large in our scale of values. Zweig has shown how much more important money has now become in the British workman's evaluation of his job. And more and more married women now go out to work. The government report states that the number of married women at work increased by thirty-nine per cent in the ten years after 1952 – to a total of one wife in three. Their motive for doing so may have been in part to find congenial company, but as research such as that by Pearl Jephcott and others at the London School of Economics has shown, it was mainly to earn more money. For the hire-purchase instalments on the new trappings of our civilization have to be paid for.

Inevitably, the emotional bond within the family has become more tenuous. With one, and often both parents eating meals in a works canteen, and with other meals often taking the form of a running buffet because of the exigencies of the working day, the family meal, as many surveys show, has begun to disappear. This, in its various forms, has always been a daily assertion of the solidarity and mutual affection of the family, and it probably has even profounder unconscious psychological significance, arising from the primitive emotions of protectiveness and loveworthiness associated with the feeding situation.

The passing of the family meal is only one indication of the present tendency for family life to become emotionally impoverished. Personal relationships between members of the family seem to be fewer and more superficial. Everybody is always going somewhere, or doing something. Some children see very little of their parents, and it seems a particular deprivation that they see so little of their mothers. The facts are attested to from a variety of sources: surveys, schoolteachers, etc. They eat their midday meal at school, and, letting themselves into the house with their own latch-keys, snatch a hasty meal in an empty house before going out to play on the streets until bedtime. Their mothers, even during the time they spend at home, have to establish a routine for getting their housework done which plays havoc with relaxed family intercourse; and when they are not working in or out of the house, they feel too much in need of rest and recreation to play the part of the loving mother very patiently or for very long. There is no suggestion that these children are neglected materially. They are better-dressed for school than were their parents as children, and are very well nourished indeed. But all this is a further manifestation of the undue emphasis placed upon material welfare. Its obverse is the loss of many of the emotional benefits which a child used to have from his home, and which he probably needs if he is to feel secure and loveworthy.

The more sombre interpretation of these facts is sometimes disputed. Fathers, it is said, spend very much more time doing jobs in the home than they did. They help with the washing-up, take the children out, and devote a good deal of their leisure time to improving and adorning their homes. This is certainly true, and yet it often looks more like a response by the husband to the practical needs of a situation in which his wife is out at work all day. If she is to get her housework done, he has to lend a hand. And with her own wage packet to support her, she is less reluctant to demand his assistance. Zweig asked the workers whom he studied how much of their leisure time was devoted to their houses and families under the headings of gardening, 'do it yourself', or home (that is family). While a large number mentioned the first two, only a very small number gave any prominence to their families as an object on which they spent their free time. Personal relationships seem here, as elsewhere, to have little chance against the imperative need for affluent display, to which work around the house makes its own contribution.

The television set has occasionally been hailed as the new cement of the family. People, it is argued, go out less in the evening than they did, but stay at home to watch television. Families visit each other in a way that had almost become old-fashioned, in order to watch television together. There is reason to question if any of this has increased the opportunities for personal contact. To sit together in silence, eyes glued to the bright screen of the television set, is hardly the optimum arrangement for enjoying each other's company. We are rarely, in spirit, even in the room at all. We are spurring our horses across the prairie under a hail of Apache arrows; or slipping quietly, with a detective, into the gangsters' hide-out, holding our breath with him to avoid discovery.

Even the wider kinship group has lost some of its cohesion. This trend was already evident a few years ago in the Young and Wilmott survey in Bethnal Green. Married couples do usually seem to maintain contact with their parents and their in-laws, but on a rather tepid basis. As Zweig puts it: 'close but not too close'.

In most discussions about such changes in the structure of the family, attention is usually focused upon the deprivations said to be caused for the children. It must not be forgotten that parents, though partly instrumental in bringing the situation about, are themselves deprived by it. As a source of mutual consolation and support the marital relationship should rank high: partners have often sought each other because their needs are thus complementary. As a setting in which all is known and therefore nothing need be concealed, it could be a haven. And the close bond with children is valuable for nurturing the self-respect and satisfying the love-needs of parents and offspring alike. Some of the results of current adult deprivations are possibly to be seen in anger and in a narcissistic emphasis upon their own well-being which makes it difficult for them to be as loving and tolerant with their children as even their changed role within the family would permit. This, according to the Eppels, is the experience our teenagers have of us as a generation.

This emotional anaemia is not confined within the family circle; an aspect of the increased money-mindedness of the workers is that personal relationships at work are no longer much valued. As Zweig's group of workers often said: 'Mates are not pals'. Contacts with neighbours are also cool. The traditional working-class community with its open doors and the warm concern of neighbours in each other's affairs, may be on its way out. The new attitude is something like this: You don't want to be unfriendly, but you do want some privacy. Zweig's observations to this effect have often been confirmed by others – most recently by Dennis in a survey on a working-class housing estate in the South of England. Dennis's comments are very germane to the argument of this chapter. While noting the decline of neighbourliness in this group he goes on to say that, as a result 'the housewife can "put on a show" of herself, her children, her way of life without being easily challenged. ... Both the failures and the successes wish to preserve the opacity of their domestic lives. The failures do not wish to be known as such. The successes do not wish to be contaminated by the failures, nor do they want to be distracted by armchair patterns of sociability and mutual aid which interfere with marital and parental goals.'

Yudkin and Holme who, if anything, are inclined to underestimate the ill-effects of such trends as these, suggest that the emotional dangers to children of mothers going to work are likely to be greater if relationships within the family are poor. The general decline in familial cohesion described above should therefore make us examine the arrangements we make for the care of especially young children while mother is out at work with a very critical eye. Grandma has been the most important resort in the past, but the weakening of the extended family tends to remove her also from the scene. Nor are neighbours (who looked after twelve per cent of the children in the Yudkin and Holme study) in the kind of community which Dennis describes going to be willing, or even asked, to assume the duty as much in the future.

The Welfare State has its substitute for maternal care in the form of the day nursery. A child in a day nursery is clean and well fed, in less danger of infection, and trained in more regular habits than might have been the case if his mother had looked after him at home instead of going out to work, but the urgent need he has for a substitute mother in the nursery, as he cannot have his own mother, receives no attention at all. He is normally looked after by a series of nurses in training, or trained nurses on a shift system, and never has the chance of learning to know and rely on a familiar person, and to feel that she has a very special interest in him. The work of Anna Freud and Dorothy Burlingham shows how great a deprivation this is felt to be by the infant himself. The evidence reviewed by Yudkin and Holme makes it clear that frequent changes in baby-minder can be very damaging; and many of the studies cited to prove the harmlessness of nurseries are from other countries, where they are run in a way which makes them more likely to meet the needs of the child. Even in such cases, however, all may not be as well as, at first sight, it seems to be. The Kibbutzim of Israel are test-cases for this. The children in a Kibbutz see a good deal of their mothers, and each is cared for, as part of a very small group, by the same nurse. Nevertheless Spiro, and more recently Bowlby, have suggested that children are not as unmarked by the experience as is sometimes assumed.

This emphasis of the day nursery service on material welfare is only one illustration of the way in which the Welfare State in general undervalues the personal element. What matters is that material privation shall be alleviated, and sometimes this is achieved not merely without gain to, but at the cost of emotional security. This is as true for example of services provided for the very old, as for those for the very young. Well-planned bungalows are provided for our old people on healthy new housing estates. Does it matter in such circumstances that they are thus carried off to the outskirts of the city, separated from their friends and neighbours and the familiar streets in which they have lived most of their lives? After all, these new bungalows are easy to clean and to manage, there are no stairs to climb, and the corporation gardens department tends the tiny lawn at the front. Municipal housing policy in general, focuses no less exclusively upon convenience and amenity. The infirm aged are looked after too, in an efficiently organized Home providing good food and comfortable living conditions. What does it matter if they are required to give up the old table or chair to which they have become so attached, for the table was rickety and the chair dirty and shabby? What does it matter if a husband and wife are separated; it is true that they have lived together for a long time and become very used to each other, but now they seem to do nothing but quarrel, and anyway organization is simpler if they are separated?

At the core of this social security system is the National Assistance Board. From the beginning its function has been defined as that of relieving material poverty. Its staff are very efficient administrators of this policy, but they and the Board have been, until very recently, largely oblivious to the more human problems which often lie behind and give rise to economic privation. Where there are such underlying problems, material relief by itself is no more than a palliative. The activities of Mr Heimler have led in the last few years to short courses on human relations for officers of the National Assistance Board, but these, though a welcome sign of changing attitudes, are still too elementary for the task which has to be performed. The Board still has fully to accept that the problems of social work are problems involving people as much as money. The new legislation for children has also, following the recommendations of the Ingleby Committee, begun to provide for preventive social work with unsatisfactory families, rather than the short-cut of removing neglected children promptly from their homes. But these are exceptions which show by contrast how very materialistic most of our public social services are.

Ronald Fletcher, comparing the sixties with the beginning of the thirties, has written: 'Surely it must be the case that the improvements in housing and material conditions made since that time have done much to improve the nature of family morals.' There is, alas, no such certainty. If evidence means anything in social affairs, it suggests that the improvement in material conditions has been accompanied by a deterioration in both inner security and outward behaviour. This does not mean that the trend towards social justice, slow and faltering enough as it is, should be halted. But we do need to recognize that we are in grave danger of satisfying the body more and more effectively at the cost of starving the emotions.

This (like the similar deprivations in slums and new housing estates) might be expected to have its greatest impact upon the lower working class, with their much greater dependence upon each other for acceptance and emotional security. Most vulnerable of all would be the working-class teenager, growing towards individuality, but facing emotional isolation as he leaves behind the children's group which has succoured him so far. But the emotional deprivations imposed by this materialism of ours extend beyond the bottom rungs of the social ladder. It is more than possible that deprivations which were once limited to the 'rough' working-class infant, are now, as more and more mothers see less and less of their babies, spreading into other classes. We may be facing in the future an expanding circle of those who are no longer able to achieve a sense of personal worthwhileness through prolonged acceptance by their parents, and are thus thrown back upon group acceptance, only to find that this also is lacking. Many of the highly responsible adults interviewed by the Eppels were perturbed by the materialist values espoused by present-day adolescents, for whom these are no more a solution than for their parents.

Societies do, of course, evolve and modify their ways of life. The changes we have witnessed since the war towards higher standards of material welfare and a greater degree of social and economic equality seem finally to be realizing many of the hopes of radical social reformers for generations past. We must not for that reason, blind ourselves to the evidence that our society may also have begun to eschew personal relationships and to cultivate hate. The economic millennium may be just around the corner, but so may be something very much less desirable. Organized societies do not easily disintegrate. The gain from human association, even on the most material level, is too great to be thrown away. Criminal and destructive tendencies will be repressed with all the weapons we have to hand. Public attitudes to criminals are toughening in a way which suggests that this process is already under way. Crime may thus be held down to a tolerable level, but the widespread yearning for social acceptance, and the need for a target on which to vent one's fury and resentment, are not to be eliminated by such means. We may expect alternative outlets to be found, including some which have been used for such purposes throughout the ages. The war mentality is one such. If the fear of, and readiness for war is constantly fed by our dammed-up inner aggressions, war itself becomes so much the more imminent.

Failing an international cataclysm we have the outgroups within our community to hate. If we cannot unite in war against a foreign enemy, we can at least join together to persecute those whom we see as the enemy in our midst. We do not need to project our imaginations too far into the future to see this happening. We have already had some experience of the facility with which group delinquency may be transformed into mass demonstrations against minority groups, as for example, at Dudley. The same tendency, however, is observable in demonstrations which seem, on the surface, to be more wholesome in character, such as those in London against the racial policies of the Fascists. To watch these demonstrations was to be made very much aware of the amount of personal aggressivity which was finding an outlet through them. Ray Gosling, in an article in *New Society*, spoke of the uncanny similarity between the reasons given by a racialist youth in Dudley for his views, and Gosling's own reason for joining C.N.D. It is as if there were a reservoir of 'free-floating hatred', which seeks expression wherever it can – and on either side of the racialist fence. Unless we do something about it, we may be on the road from an affluent materialism in which older social divisions have lost much of their meaning, to a deprived society which can contain its deprivations only by dividing on a new basis, between the haters and the hated.

But perhaps our fate will not be as dramatic as this. Perhaps we shall express our discontentment only in the further accumulation of less obvious symptoms such as marital disharmony, alcoholism, gambling, and sexual promiscuity. Indices for all of these as well as for crime are on the increase in our affluent society. The extraordinary efflorescence of Bingo Clubs and Casinos, though not in itself a matter for concern, may become so if it is seen as an aspect of something more serious, as an ineffective attempt to assuage emotional disquiet through dreams of sudden affluence. The fact that illegitimate births increased by thirty per cent between 1953 and 1963 (in spite of the wide knowledge nowadays about contraception) and that over one third of all teenage brides are already pregnant, may suggest similarly a drive towards sensual gratification divested of personal content, which (as in the case of the substitute satisfaction of the deprived child) is likely to become compulsive because it is not what is really being sought. Our future may be marked by heroic decline, or may merely begin to curl at the edges; what is most unlikely, if the preceding analysis is correct, is that we shall escape scot-free.

That analysis is, of course, highly hypothetical. It has nevertheless, a good deal of surface plausibility. It refers to the kind of development which many sociologists have described since Tönnies presented his classical account of the trend in modern societies from *Gemeinschaft* to *Gesellschaft*. In the language of the courts, a *prima facie* case can be made out for it; and we cannot risk the possibility that it may be true, and that we have done nothing about it. Research on the relationship between emotional deprivation and current changes in social values is urgently needed. We need also to do some serious research to determine what connexion if any exists between these changes, and present trends in alcoholism, gambling, teenage delinquency, etc. In spite of the vital importance of this issue, solid factual information about it is almost entirely lacking.

The disease, if it exists, will not be easy to isolate and describe; finding a cure is bound to be even more difficult. There is no question of putting the clock back. Affluence and a greater degree of equality are here to stay and ought to be extended. Nor do we want to return to the kind of family in which wives were confined to the home, dependent for every penny they received upon the goodwill of their husbands. At times like this the would-be reformer usually resorts to a convenient evasion, that a solution must be found in education. In this case, there may be too much at stake for us to be content with any kind of evasion. The problem often lies further back than school, and being emotional in character, has little or nothing to do with the accumulation of facts or even the receiving of moral instruction. If education is implicated, it is education defined very much more widely than usual. Learning is involved, but it is the learning which takes place in the course of our personal intercourse with other people, and especially with our parents, as a result of which we build up a picture of ourselves as basically loveworthy (or not), and acquire a habitual reaction to those other people, of confidence and acceptance (or the contrary) as a result. Perhaps it would be a good thing if this kind of education played a more prominent part (or even any part at all) in our classroom curricula.

It would be helpful if there were such a recognition of the importance of personal relationships at the level of public policy alone. In the age of the Welfare State, the state is the most widely influential agent at work in the community. What it does has an effect in every corner of our national life. If our social services, for children, for old people, for the sick, or for the poor, were infused with as much concern for the emotional as for the material needs of their clients, a powerful leaven in the right direction would have begun.

Here and there some progress is to be discerned. The first, though inadequate, measures adopted by the National Assistance Board have already been mentioned. The Children's Act 1963, in its first section, recognizes the primary importance of healing the family situations of deprived children if this is at all possible – a welcome relief for children's departments, who have been trying for years to do just this in spite of laws which saw them as mainly concerned with *rescuing* children from their unsatisfactory homes. The danger of separating the sick infant from his mother has been seen also to be achieving more recognition from hospital authorities. The abolition of the discharged prisoner's aid societies is another sound step, for as a group (with a few exceptions) they epitomize the over-emphasis of material as compared with psychological and social help.

Much more, however, still remains to be done : in the care of the aged and the disabled, in housing, in the National Health Service, and in public health, for instance. And the changes called for will only occur if the professional training of the workers in these services is modified appropriately.

Of all the welfare experts who are implicated in this problem, none has greater responsibility than the medical profession. Mental health needs to take its place side by side with physical health as a main concern of doctors and nurses, and this means a substantial reorientation of training in these fields. This would be bound, ultimately, to have its effect upon a wide range of services in which health considerations are to the fore. Especially valuable would be such knowledge on the part of health visitors, and the doctors and nurses in child welfare centres. They are dealing with mothers and children at the crucial early stages in their development together; when mothers, faced with current problems posed for them by their own feelings and those of their children, are most strongly motivated towards achieving understanding.

The crime problem, it has been suggested, is very complicated. Many causes are at work, intricately interwoven one with another. We cannot afford to abandon the analysis of this aetiological complex, although its elucidation may take a very long time. Meanwhile, it is open to us to take some action of a prophylactic kind. For if we wait until all is known, we may wait too long.

Further Reading

The only British book dealing with the whole field is the author's *Crime and the Penal System*, University Tutorial Press (2nd edition), 1962. In addition, reference may be made to the following:

Chapter 1

BAGOT, J. H., *Juvenile Delinquency*, Cape, 1941

GRUNHUT, MAX., *Juvenile Offenders Before the Courts*, O.U.P., 1956

HAVARD, J. D. J., *The Detection of Secret Homicide*, Macmillan, 1960

HOME OFFICE, *Report of the Committee on Homosexual Offences and Prostitution* (The Wolfenden Report), Cmnd 247, H.M.S.O., 1957

HOME OFFICE, *Criminal Statistics*, Annual volumes, H.M.S.O.

JONES, HOWARD, 'The Rural Offender in England', *Bulletin of the International Society of Criminology*, 2nd Semester, 1958

MANNHEIM, HERMANN, *Social Aspects of Crime in England Between the Wars*, pp. 36 ff., Allen and Unwin, 1940

MANNHEIM, KARL, *Diagnosis of Our Time*, Ch. III, Routledge and Kegan Paul, 1943

MARTIN, J. P., *Offenders as Employees*, Macmillan, 1962

McCLINTOCK, F. H., and GIBSON, E., *Robbery in London*, Chs. 1–3, Macmillan, 1961

Chapter 2

BENNEY, MARK, *Low Company*, Peter Davies, 1936

COHEN, ALBERT K., *Delinquent Boys*, Routledge and Kegan Paul, 1956

CLOWARD, R. A., and OHLIN, L. E., *Delinquency and Opportunity*, Routledge and Kegan Paul, 1961

JONES, HOWARD, 'Approaches to an Ecological Study', *British Journal of Delinquency*, Vol. 8, 1958

KERR, MADELINE, *The People of Ship Street*, Routledge and Kegan Paul, 1958

LANDER, BERNARD, *Towards an Understanding of Juvenile Delinquency*, Columbia, 1954

MAYS, JOHN B., *Growing Up in the City*, Liverpool University Press, 1954

MORRIS, TERENCE P., *The Criminal Area*, Routledge and Kegan Paul, 1957

SPINLEY, BETTY M., *The Deprived and the Privileged*, Routledge and Kegan Paul, 1953

VOLD, GEORGE B., *Theoretical Criminology*, Ch. XI, Oxford (New York), 1958

WILSON, HARRIETT, *Delinquency and Child Neglect*, Allen and Unwin, 1962

YOUNG, MICHAEL, and WILMOTT, PETER, *Family and Kinship in East London*, Routledge and Kegan Paul, 1957

Chapter 3

GLUECK, S. and E. T., *Physique and Delinquency*, Harper, 1956

SHELDON, W. H., *Varieties of Delinquent Youth*, Harper, 1949

WOLFGANG, M. E., 'Cesare Lombroso 1835–1909', in *Pioneers in Criminology* (ed. H. Mannheim), Stevens, 1960

WHEELAN, LORNA, 'Aggressive Psychopathy in One of a Pair of Uniovular Twins', *British Journal of Delinquency*, Vol. 2, 1951

WOODWARD, M., *The Role of Low Intelligence in Delinquency*, Institute for the Study and Treatment of Delinquency

Chapters 4 and 5

ABRAHAMSEN, DAVID, *The Psychology of Crime*, Columbia, 1960

AICHHORN, AUGUST, *Wayward Youth*, Imago, 1951

BOWLBY, JOHN, *Forty-four Juvenile Thieves*, Baillière, Tindall & Cox, 1946

BROWN, J. A. C., *Freud and the Post-Freudians*, Penguin, 1961

DU BOIS, C., in Kardiner, Abraham, *Psychological Frontiers of Society*, Columbia, 1959

FLUGEL, J. C., *Man, Morals and Society*, Duckworth, 1945

FREUD, SIGMUND, *Psychopathology of Everyday Life*, Benn, 1956
Two Short Accounts of Psycho-Analysis, Penguin, 1962

Further Reading

GIBBENS, T. C. N., and PRINCE, JOYCE, *Shoplifting*, Institute for the Study and Treatment of Delinquency, 1962

HALL, CALVIN S., *Primer of Freudian Psychology*, Mentor Books, 1958

HEALY, W., and BRONNER, A. F., *New Light on Delinquency and its Treatment*, Yale, 1946

HOME OFFICE, *Report of the Committee on Children and Young Persons* (The Ingleby Report), Cmnd 1191, H.M.S.O., 1960

JONES, HOWARD, *Alcoholic Addiction*, Chs. V–VII, Tavistock, 1963

ROBERTSON, JAMES, *Young Children in Hospital*, Tavistock, 1958

WAY, LEWIS, *Adler and his Psychology*, Penguin, 1956

WOOTTON, BARONESS, *Social Science and Social Pathology*, Ch. IV, Allen & Unwin, 1959

ZILBOORG, GREGORY, *Psychology of the Criminal Act and Punishment*, Hogarth, 1955

Chapter 6

BOWLBY, JOHN, op. cit.

CLOWARD and OHLIN, op. cit.

CRESSEY, DONALD R., *Other People's Money*, Free Press, 1953

COHEN, ALBERT K., op. cit.

ELKIN, W. A., *The English Penal System*, Penguin, 1957

GIBBENS, T. C. N., *Psychiatric Studies of Borstal Lads*, O.U.P., 1963

HAMMOND, W. H., and CHEYEN, EDNA, *Persistent Criminals*, H.M.S.O., 1963

JONES, HOWARD, 'Policemen as Social Workers', *New Society*, 14 November 1963

LOMBROSO, CESARE, *Le Crime: Causes et Remèdes*, 1899

MACK, JOHN A., 'Police Juvenile Liaison Schemes', *British Journal of Criminology*, Vol. 3, 1963

McCLINTOCK, F. H., *Attendance Centres*, Macmillan, 1961

SHELDON, W. H., op. cit.

SLATER, ELIOT, *Neurotic and Psychotic Illnesses in Twins*, H.M.S.O., 1953

SUTHERLAND, E. H., and CRESSEY, DONALD R., *Principles of Criminology*, Lippincott, 1960

TANNENBAUM, FRANK, *Crime and the Community*, Ginn, 1938

U.K. GOVERNMENT, *Annual Reports of H. M. Commissioners of Prisons*, H.M.S.O.

WEST, D. J., *The Habitual Prisoner*, Macmillan, 1963

Chapter 7

EWING, A. C., *The Morality of Punishment*, Kegan Paul, 1929

FLUGEL, J. C., op. cit.

GOODHART, A. L., *English Law and the Moral Law*, Stevens, 1953

HOBHOUSE, L. T., *Elements of Social Justice*, Allen & Unwin, 1930, Ch. VI

LONGFORD, LORD, *The Idea of Punishment*, Chapman, 1961

MANNHEIM, HERMANN, *The Dilemma of Penal Reform*, Allen & Unwin, 1939

ROSE, GORDON, *The Struggle for Penal Reform*, Stevens, 1961

TEMPLE, ARCHBISHOP, *The Ethics of Penal Action*, Clarke Hall Fellowship, 1934

TUTTLE, ELIZABETH O., *The Crusade Against Capital Punishment in Great Britain*, Stevens, 1961

VOLD, G. B., *Theoretical Criminology*, op. cit.

WOOTTON, BARONESS, op. cit., Ch. 8

ZILBOORG, GREGORY, op. cit.

Chapter 8

GLUECK, S. and E. T., *Predicting Delinquency and Crime*, Harvard, 1959

HOME OFFICE, *Report of the Committee on Children and Young Persons* (The Ingleby Report), Cmnd 1191, H.M.S.O., 1960

HOME OFFICE, *Murder*, H.M.S.O., 1961

HOME OFFICE, *Report of the Committee on the Business of the Criminal Courts* (The Streatfeild Report), Cmnd 1289, 1961

HOOD, ROGER, *Sentencing in Magistrates' Courts*, Stevens, 1962

MANNHEIM, H., and WILKINS, L. T., *Prediction Methods in Relation to Borstal Training*, H.M.S.O., 1955

MANNHEIM, HERMANN, *Courts for Adolescents*, Institute for the Study and Treatment of Delinquency, 1958

NATIONAL PROBATION AND PAROLE ASSOCIATION (U.S.A.), 'Disposition and Treatment' in *The Problem of Delinquency* (ed. S. and E. T. Glueck), pp. 580 ff., Houghton Mifflin, 1959

NYQUIST, OLA, *Juvenile Justice*, Macmillan, 1960.

PIHLBLAD, C. T., 'The Juvenile Offender in Norway', *The Problem of Delinquency*, loc. cit., pp. 313 ff.

TAPPAN, PAUL W., 'Young Adults Under the Youth Authority', in *The Indeterminate Sentence*, ibid. pp. 521 ff., United Nations, 1954.

Further Reading

Chapter 9

BASOLO, J. C. G., *The Integration of Prison Labour with the National Economy*, United Nations, 1960

BISHOP, NORMAN, 'Group Work at Pollington Borstal', *Howard Journal*, 10, n. 3, 1960

ELKIN, W. A., op. cit.

GITTINS, JOHN, *Approved School Boys*, H.M.S.O., 1952

HOME OFFICE, *Work for Prisoners*, Cmnd 4462, H.M.S.O., 1933
The Organization of After-care. Report of the Advisory Council on the Treatment of Offenders, H.M.S.O., 1963

HOWARD, D. L., *The English Prisons*, Methuen, 1960

JONES, HOWARD, *Reluctant Rebels*, Tavistock, 1961
Prison Reform Now, Fabian Society, 1959
'The Problem of After-care', *British Journal of Criminology*, IV, 1964

KLARE, HUGH J., *The Anatomy of Prison*, Penguin, 1962

MILLER, DEREK, *Growth to Freedom*, Tavistock, 1964

MORRIS, TERENCE and PAULINE, assisted by Barbara Barer, *Pentonville: a Sociological Study of an English Prison*, Routledge and Kegan Paul, 1963

SYKES, GRESHAM, M., *The Society of Captives*, Princeton University, 1958

Chapter 10

ALINSKY, SAUL D., *Reveille for Radicals*, Chicago, 1945

HERBERT, W. L., and JARVIS, F. V., *Dealing with Delinquents*, Methuen, 1961

HOME OFFICE, *Report of the Committee on the Probation Service* (The Morrison Report), Cmnd 1650, H.M.S.O., 1962

HOME OFFICE, *Groupwork in Probation*, 1966

JONES, HOWARD, 'The Group Approach to Treatment', *Howard Journal*, Vol. II, No. 1, 1962

KING, JOAN F. S. (ed.), *The Probation Service*, Butterworth, 1958

KOBRIN, SOLOMON, 'The Chicago Area Project: Twenty-five Year Assessment', *Annals of the American Academy of Political and Social Science*, No. 332, 1959

RADZINOWICZ, L. (ed.), *The Results of a Probation*, Macmillan, 1958

SPENCER, J. C., *Stress and Release on a Housing Estate*, Tavistock, 1964

UNITED NATIONS, *Probation and Related Measures*, 1951

Chapter 11

COHEN, ALBERT K., op. cit.

CLOWARD & OHLIN, op. cit.

CRAWFORD, P., MALAMUD, D. J., and DUMPSON, J. R., *Working with Teenage Gangs*, Welfare Council of New York, 1950

EDUCATION, MINISTRY OF, *Report of the Committee on the Youth Service in England and Wales* (The Albemarle Report), Cmnd 929, H.M.S.O., 1960

EPPEL, E. M. and M., 'Connotations of Morality', *British Journal of Sociology*, XIII, 1962

FYVEL, T. R., *The Insecure Offenders*, Chatto & Windus, 1961

GIBBENS, T. C. N. *Psychiatric Studies of Borstal Lads*, O.U.P., 1963

HARLOW, H. F., and M. K., 'Social Deprivation in Monkeys', *Scientific American*, November 1962

JONES, HOWARD, *Alcoholic Addiction*, op. cit. Chs. 8 and 13

MARTIN, J. M., *Juvenile Vandalism*, Charles C. Thomas, 1961

MCCLINTOCK, F. H., et al., *Crimes of Violence*, especially Appendix XI, Macmillan, 1963

MEAD, MARGARET, *Coming of Age in Samoa*, Penguin, 1963

MIDDENDORF, WOLF, *New Forms of Juvenile Delinquency*, United Nations, 1960

REDL, FRITZ, 'Psychology of Gang Formation', *Psycho-analytic Study of the Child*, Imago, 1945

SCOTT, PETER, 'Gangs and Delinquent Groups in London', *British Journal of Delinquency*, VII, 1956

THRASHER, F. M., *The Gang*, University of Chicago, 1947

TURNER, MERFYN, L., *Ship Without Sails*, University of London, 1953

ZWEIG, F., *The Worker in an Affluent Society*, Heinemann, 1961

Chapter 12

BOWLBY, JOHN, *Child Care and the Growth of Love*, Penguin, 1963
'Children in the Kibbutz', *Guardian*, 3 July 1963

DENNIS, NORMAN, 'Who Needs Neighbours?', *New Society*, 25 July 1963

EPPEL, E. M., and M., loc. cit.

FLETCHER, RONALD, *The Family and Marriage*, Penguin, 1962

FREUD, A., and BURLINGHAM, D., *Infants Without Families*, Allen & Unwin, 1947

FYVEL, T. R., op. cit.

Further Reading

GALBRAITH, J. K., *The Affluent Society*, Penguin, 1962

GLUECK, SHELDON, 'Theory and Fact in Criminology', *The Problem of Delinquency*, loc cit.

GOSLING, RAY, 'Twistings in that Poor White Boy', *New Society*, 29 November 1962

HEIMLER, EUGENE, 'Looking Behind Cold Facts', *New Society*, 18 April 1963

HENDERSON, SIR DAVID K., *Psychopathic States*, 1939

HOME OFFICE, *Report of the Committee on Children and Young Persons* (The Ingleby Report), Cmnd 1191, 1960

JEPHCOTT, PEARL, et al., *Married Women Working*, Allen & Unwin, 1962

LYNES, TONY, 'Poverty in the Welfare State', *Aspect*, August 1963

PACKARD, VANCE, *The Hidden Persuaders*, Penguin, 1962

SHELDON, W. H., op. cit.

TÖNNIES, F., Community and Association, Routledge and Kegan Paul, 1955

TOWNSEND, PETER, *The Last Refuge*, Routledge and Kegan Paul, 1962

U.K. GOVERNMENT, 'Social Changes in Britain: A Government Survey', reprinted in *New Society*, 27 December 1962

UNITED NATIONS, *Report on the Second U.N. Congress, 1960, on the Prevention of Crime and the Treatment of Offenders*, 1961

VOLD, G. B., op. cit.

WOOTTON, BARONESS, op. cit. Ch. II

YOUNG, MICHAEL, and WILMOTT, PETER, op. cit.

YUDKIN, SIMON, and HOLME, ANTHEA, *Working Mothers and their Children*, Michael Joseph, 1963

ZWEIG, F., op. cit.

Index

171

Index

Index